FIRST MOMENTS OF SELF-AWARENESS IN CHILDHOOD

This thought-provoking volume explores the phenomenon of childhood experiences of sudden moments of self-awareness. Locating them as meaningful developmental events, it draws on, and is illustrated by, detailed analysis of individuals' narratives of inner experience and recollections of childhood.

Uniquely highlighting the relevant writings of literary figures such as C.G. Jung, Vladimir Nabokov, Ian McEwan, and Henning Mankell, Dolph Kohnstamm explores the construction of selfhood, and the effects it has on time, space, and the other. Together with a chapter assessing the role of the default brain network in the development of self-conception, it both supports and challenges theories of development.

First Moments of Self-awareness in Childhood offers a new conception of children's development of a sense of individuality and will be of great interest to scholars and students of psychology, philosophy, and sociology.

Dolph Kohnstamm is Professor Emeritus in Developmental Psychology, Leiden University, Netherlands. He is the author of works including *Parental Descriptions of Child Personality*, *Temperament in Context*, and *Jean Piaget, Children and the Class-Inclusion Problem*.

FIRST MOMENTS OF SELF-AWARENESS IN CHILDHOOD

A Phenomenological Approach

Dolph Kohnstamm

Routledge
Taylor & Francis Group
LONDON AND NEW YORK

First published 2022

by Routledge
2 Park Square, Milton Park, Abingdon, Oxon OX14 4RN

and by Routledge
605 Third Avenue, New York, NY 10158

Routledge is an imprint of the Taylor & Francis Group, an informa business

British Library Cataloguing-in-Publication Data
A catalogue record for this book is available from the British Library

Library of Congress Cataloging-in-Publication Data
A catalog record for this book has been requested

ISBN: 978-0-367-75202-6 (hbk)
ISBN: 978-0-367-75204-0 (pbk)
ISBN: 978-1-003-16147-9 (ebk)

Typeset in Bembo
by Apex CoVantage, LLC

I want to express my gratitude toward all those who sent me a depiction of their very personal memories in good faith. In virtually all cases, I was the first one for whom they wrote down their experiences, which they had saved for so long.

CONTENTS

I AM I

This book is a fully revised and extended edition of *I am I, the discovery of the self*, which was first published by De Bezige Bij (2002), followed for a number of years by Amsterdam University Press, and by bravenewbooks.nl since 2015.

In 2007 an English translation was published by what used to be Athena Press (London). It was published in German by Hans Huber (Bern) and in Japanese.

A Mandarin translation by Zhang Yuqin, professor of psychology at the Chinese Academy of Sciences, was published in 2020 by Oriental Press (Beijing and Hong Kong).

After the publication of *I am I*, I received many new memories by mail or email, and in the form of locations in (auto)biographies. I have included here many of those besides the ones I already had in my collection. In addition, I wrote a new chapter (15) on interesting modern neuropsychological research related to my topic.

This book serves as the conclusion of a project I have been working on since my retirement in 1997.

Dolph Kohnstamm
Amsterdam, October 2020

FOREWORD

This book is powerful in unique ways. Several years before it was written, the author, Dolph Kohnstamm, first told me about the phenomenon of sudden awareness of self. Because of my deep respect for Dolph's scholarship, I kept listening but remained skeptical about this particular topic. The phenomenon of sudden awareness of self did not map onto my own past studies of children's development. I've always been more interested in observable behavior, especially behavior studied prospectively, than reports of inner experience and recollections of childhood. Nor did the 'I-am-me' topic resonate particularly with my personal experience. In fact, I haven't been able to remember a time when I was unaware of being a separate person. But when I finally started to read this book, I became increasingly fascinated. I began to understand Dolph's enthusiasm. And in the end, I saw the book as a unique window into a very interesting phenomenon. How did my response change so completely?

First, the stories that are the core of the book have a cumulative power. These narratives come mostly from ordinary but literate people who, responding to Dolph's interest in the topic, sent him letters. Some are from the writings of well-known literary figures, such as C.G. Jung and, in the newest edition of the book, Henning Mankell. I found the book's first few stories somewhat intriguing. And, as the few stories became many, I was surprised to find that I had become completely absorbed. The stories all touch a common theme of awakening to one's individuality. At the same time, however, they have so many distinctive elements and are told in such authentic voices that they add up to an impressively rich description of the phenomenon. The stories show a wonderful burst of simultaneous awareness of the self, the not-self, and the physical environment. They give a sense of the person experiencing a sharp and profound separation from others. Such an experience could sound pathological, but in most stories the flavor is, instead, the opposite of pathological. It's often an intense, highly valued, ultimately enriching experience. So, as I read this book, I was getting hooked on something phenomenological in ways that I hadn't been for decades, if ever. I was becoming convinced that this burst of self-awareness is a meaningful kind of developmental event.

The collection of stories provides some support for theories of development, as well as, perhaps, some mild challenges. For example, developmental psychologists typically expect that children are able to form stable self-identities only after they are cognitively capable of holding two dimensions in mind at the same time. Somewhere around ages 6 to 8, kids are able to consistently recognize that a transformed physical object has the same matter as before the transformation, such as a ball of clay flattened into a pancake has the same amount of clay as when it was in a ball. As Piaget explained, kids at that age are able to keep horizontal and vertical dimensions in mind at the same time, and not be overwhelmed by the sensory power of one dimension over another. Likewise, at around this same time, children appear to be capable of thinking, in consistent ways, about how others perceive them as distinct individuals. But here's a theoretical challenge posed by the book: a number of the narratives convincingly describe self-insight experiences that happen much earlier in life. We no longer think that cognitive development stages rigidly conform to particular ages, but it's still interesting to wonder how such a sophisticated awareness of one's self as distinct from others might form in very early childhood. I could give a number of other examples of how Dolph has pulled important themes from the collection of stories. One of the most moving was how the experiences in the stories sometimes reflect a realization of life's transience and a way of coping with it.

With all the richness of its collection of narratives and its light sprinkling of scientific knowledge about psychological development, this book opens a vista. It does not put the 'I-am-me' phenomenon into a pretty box and close the lid. This book is not a lecture. It is what I imagine a scientific-literary salon might be like. We readers have been invited, along with other intellectually vibrant participants, to the elegantly fashionable

Kohnstamm home, to sip tea and encounter a succession of thoughtful stories and ideas about the stories. As we form questions and reactions in our minds, some answers appear upon turning the page. Others are left for our own explorations, maybe to be discussed at the next meeting.

Professor John E. Bates, PhD
Department of Psychological and Brain Sciences,
Indiana University, Bloomington, Indiana USA

1

THE DEVELOPMENT OF SELF-AWARENESS

For centuries, scholars have been racking their brains over the question how phenomena like self-awareness and self-conception are possible. The capacity to think about yourself – self-reflection – is an aspect of what is currently called 'meta-cognition': knowledge about knowledge, 'super-knowledge', as it were.

Awareness can rise above the ability to think by formulating thoughts about this ability and expressing these if necessary.

An uncle of mine toured America from East to West and back for a year when he was a 24-year-old student. His last letter before he returned to the Netherlands started as follows:

> Now that I am walking on the familiar streets of Washington again, I often look at myself and wonder: how have you changed [because of the trip DK]?[1]

Most people are able to think about themselves. We say things like: 'I was wrong', or 'That was stupid of me', or, worse: 'I was not myself, Your Honor, I did not know what I was doing'. These are all expressions by someone who says something about his own person.

Apparently, people feel like they consist of two 'selves'. A 'self' who has done something or wants something, who believes something, and another 'self' who remarks on this, who wants to oppose this, who is proud of this. However, I believe it is better not to refer to the existence of two 'selves', but about two parts of one Self.

A century ago, the American psychologist William James – who is considered the founder of modern psychology – determined that these two parts should best be referred to as 'I' and 'Me'. The *I* is the subject, the observing part of the Self, and the *Me* is the object, the objectively observed part. James believed that only the objective Self could be known and studied, and that the subjective Self could not.[2]

Whatever the case may be, the fact is that we consider talking about two different forms of 'I' very natural: the acting 'I' (feeling, pursuing, being ill, etc.) and the 'I' that reflects on this, and which has an opinion about this acting, feeling, and thinking: 'I often look at myself and wonder: how have you changed?'

The 'Me' as conceptualized by James can think, but not about itself. If it would do so, it would turn into the 'I'. This means that the 'Me' is not self-reflexive. Only the 'I' can think about a whole range of things, including about the 'Me'. The question is whether it can also think about itself as the subject. After all, once the 'I' does so, it makes itself the object of its own thoughts.

But how is it possible that I can think something like this? How can people become aware of this duality within themselves? The fields of philosophy and psychology spent a lot of time in search of an answer to this question.

Nowadays, it is up to neuroscientists to find an explanation for this miracle of human awareness. Many have come close, thanks to their knowledge of our brains and their intuition. I consider the most important among them to be the Portuguese-American biologist and neuropsychologist Antonio Damasio, professor in neuroscience at the University of Southern California.

With his background in psychology, he searches for the foundation of this process in the evolutionary development of feelings and emotions, which has lasted for millions for years and during which humanity was the only species in which 'the Self became the witness of the mind'. This development resulted in the creation of neurological mechanisms that made this possible. And if these were found not to contribute to the survival of the homo species, they disappeared:

> "For millions of years, numerous creatures had active minds, but only in those that developed a Self which was found to be able to act as a witness of the mind was the existence of this active mind acknowledged. And only once the mind had developed the language to express this, was it generally admitted that the mind exists. The

> Self as a witness is a supplementary feature present in each of us, and exposes events we call 'mental'."[3]

The evolutionary development started with what Damasio calls a 'protoself', followed by a 'core self' from which the Self ultimately develops into an 'autobiographical self', of which this book attests in every possible way. The earliest two phases did not yet involve any thoughts about the own mind, as became the case in later self-reflection. In the preliminary stages of the protoself and the core self, humankind did not yet have a language with words and phrases. People could only express their feelings and emotions using guttural sounds, gestures, posture, and facial expressions. However, there will likely have been proper observers in these two stages who were able to derive feelings and emotions like anger, happiness, and sadness from this 'physical language'.

But in Western philosophy and philosophical ideas about the self and self-awareness, people paid little attention to the development of this self-awareness during *childhood and school years* for centuries. This was likely in part due to the belief that our body housed an immortal soul that was considered the core and essence of ourselves. If this soul is timeless and immortal, it does not need to develop from *nothing* into *something*, as it would already be present upon our birth and reside in our body until our death.

Even Rousseau, who can be considered one of the first developmental psychologists with his *Emile* novel, did not use his book to discuss the question how children can develop thoughts about themselves, in other words, how they develop a self-image or self-concept.

The self of a newborn baby does not yet consist of more than the merely physical sensations of his or her own body: pleasant sensations – such as a caress, comfortable warmth, and drinking delicious milk – and unpleasant sensations – such as hunger, cold, pain, and tiredness. It would actually be better not to use the term 'self' yet because there is no sense yet of unity experienced in a conscious manner. But these first pleasant and unpleasant sensations do in part contribute to the first steps toward what will grow into self-awareness. The Dutch psychiatrist and author Frederik van Eeden (1860–1932) wrote:

> "Nobody of us can say when he started feeling like 'I'. I do not remember anything about my feelings as a newborn, as an embryo, but it must have been a sense of being. It would only have been a very small, primitive spark, which slowly grew into a realm of light."[4]

But how to proceed? How does this spark grow?

After a few months, the physical awareness – the 'physical self' – will already consist of more: seeing, hearing, and recognizing events in which the baby plays an active role. Moving hands are a striking example of this. These hands initially do not have any meaning for the baby in relation to the self. They are of the same category as the mobile above the crib. Babies can be enticed looking at their moving hands as they move in and out of their field of vision. Their tiny brains are not yet able to establish a connection between moving and seeing.

But at some point in the early development of their brains, there is a moment when they get the impression that they can move or hold their hands still themselves while looking at them. And that the mobile does not move spontaneously, but only if they hit it with their hand. While observing the world, in a baby grows an early sense of itself, which already consists of more than just pleasant and unpleasant sensations, and which gradually grows into a (physical) self and a non-self.

Spatial observations also play a role in this 'sense of self'. This concerns how children experience their body amidst other people and objects – close by or far away, touching or not touching, and how this sensation changes when they roll over, crawl, or turn their heads. This also creates a 'sense of self', an internal model, a form of core knowledge.

Later, 'possessions' start to play a role: 'mine!' This is a start of 'me-knowledge', potentially accompanied by feelings of pride when achieving things and moving from the safe bond with the parents toward increasing independence.

This is how self-awareness and the ability for self-reflection develop gradually. An autobiographical memory arises: the ability to reflect on and think ahead about events in which I was or will be involved.

But mental leaps do occur, leading to *sudden* self-awareness.

A German teacher wrote about a memory back from when she was 4 or 5 years old:

> "I was sitting in the garden on a summer day. The older children had gone to school. I had put some lettuce in a shoe box and placed a number of snails on it. When I looked at them and wondered what they would do, I realized that I would in all my life never know what it would be like to be a snail. At the same time, I became overwhelmingly aware of myself ['spürte ich mich selbst'], of my body, of the fact that I was alive, of what I was feeling, of the sun on my back, of the fabric of my dress on my skin, of the wind in my hair,

of the sand on my hands. And I was suddenly filled with the greatest sensation of happiness: I am, I feel myself, I do what I want to do, I am internal and external. This event faded over the course of time, but it never disappeared entirely."

This book discusses such mental leaps.

Notes

1 Dolph Kohnstamm, editor (2001) *Still No War: A Correspondence between Two Dutchmen: Son Max and Father Philip Kohnstamm 1938–1939*. London, Athena Press.
2 William James (1890) *The Principles of Psychology Volume One*. New York, Holt & Co. Authorized edition (2014) New York, Dover Publications Inc.
3 Antonio Damasio (2010) *Self Comes to Mind: Constructing the Conscious Brain*. New York, Pantheon Books.
4 Frederik van Eeden (1915/2011) *Bij het licht van de oorlogsvlam*. Amsterdam, Versluys.

2

SUDDEN INSIGHT

One of the most miraculous things a child can experience is the sudden realization of being an independent individual. This can stand out as a new and impressive insight in its conscious mind. It can impress children who experience such insight so much that both the thought and the sensation of that moment, as well as the situation in which it occurred, are engraved into their memories and stay there for years, sometimes even well into their old age.

It is a sudden flash of self-awareness. The later memory of such sudden insight is something different from an *earliest memory*. Everyone has a first or oldest memory, often of an event from their daily lives which in itself is not very important. These earliest memories often stem from our third year, but there are also people who have memories from their second year, as well as people who cannot remember anything from before their fifth year. An earliest memory is usually quite trivial, even though it is valuable to the person cherishing it.

The sudden flashes of insight discussed in this book often occur later in the life of a child, approximately after its fourth year, and sometimes only during its adolescence. But this book also contains a few memories of children who were hardly four years old when they suddenly experienced themselves as individuals because of a certain trigger.

There are only a few adults who remember such a moment of clear insight from their childhood. But there are many more of them than we realized until this moment. This has become clear from numerous letters and emails I received. Many of these writers believed that they were the only ones with such a remarkable memory. They had never read anything or heard anyone talk about it.

How did they end up sending me their memories?

Halfway through the 1970s, a Swedish friend of mine showed me an interview with the famous Swiss psychiatrist Carl G. Jung broadcast by the BBC. The interview was conducted in the summer of 1959 when Jung was 84 years old. This interview sparked my interest in a phenomenon that became my main interest in psychology for many years, finally resulting in this book. (I advise readers of this book to listen to this discussion, in particular to the first seven minutes in which he tells about his 'I am I' moment.)[1]

The interview started as follows:

"INTERVIEWER: Do you remember the moment at which you first had a moment of self-awareness?

JUNG: I was eleven years old when I suddenly, whilst on my way to school, stepped out from the fog. It was like I had been walking around in fog, and when I stepped out of it, I knew that 'I am': I am what I am. And then I thought: but what was I *before* this time? That's when I realized I had been living in fog, where I could not see the difference between myself and things. I was simply a thing among other things.

INTERVIEWER: Was this because you were going through a special episode in your life, or was it simply like those things that happen during adolescence?

JUNG: That is difficult to say. Insofar as I can remember, nothing had happened prior to this which could explain this sudden state of awareness.

INTERVIEWER: Could you possibly have had an argument with your parents?

JUNG: No, no!"

I do not know why this fragment in particular made such an impression on me. Did I recognize something from my own youth in it? I do have some vague memories of two events that were a bit similar, but these similarities were evidently not significant enough to cause a 'shock of recognition'.

However, I kept thinking about what Jung had said, and suddenly I got the idea that if he had such an experience, there might be more people with a similar memory in their mind. I had a biweekly column in a daily newspaper at that time and decided to ask my readers. Within two weeks,

I had received 20 responses with descriptions of sudden mental leaps in the way people thought about themselves during their childhoods. That is how my collection was born.

However, if I am so interested in sudden flashes of insight of children, would it not have been better to ask children themselves? After all, now I had to depend on what adults believed they remembered from long ago, and everyone knows how events from the past can be distorted. However, I faced the issue of having to conduct interviews with many, many children, maybe even a couple of thousand, to ultimately end up with a dozen usable descriptions. I also did not know in advance which age I should focus on, which is something I could not have known, because, to my knowledge, similar studies have never been conducted.

I gradually received more descriptions of similar experiences, and numerous people pointed out such childhood memories in novels and autobiographies of authors.

The next chapter will discuss the latter.

Note

1 YouTube *Carl Jung and Face to Face.*

3

SUDDEN SELF-AWARENESS AMONG AUTHORS

In his book about Baudelaire, author and philosopher Jean-Paul Sartre wrote:

> "Each of us experienced the accidental and shocking moment of self-awareness in his youth."[1]

I do not believe that 'each of us' experienced something like this in his youth, as Sartre alleged. I know too many people who cannot remember anything about a sudden flash of self-awareness to accept this idea. Whenever I ask adults if they remember something like this, among the many people who read or hear my question, only a few can offer a confirming and convincing answer. And, to the best of my knowledge, scientific literature does not contain any references to this unique 'flash' phenomenon. A young woman concluded the description of her memory as follows:

> "In response to your book and my own memory, I have sometimes asked others whether they there familiar with such a moment. I found out that the world divides itself into two when asked such a question. Those who are familiar with it, and those who do not and have no clue what you are talking about."

However, I owe a first description of childhood self-discovery in literature to Sartre. This description is offered by Richard Hughes in his novel *A High Wind in Jamaica.*

Richard Hughes (1900–1976)

> "And suddenly, something very important happened to Emily. She suddenly realized who she was. It is most likely complete happenstance that this did not happen five years earlier, or five years later [when Emily is 10 years old DK], and it certainly happened without any reason that afternoon. She had been playing in a corner of the bow, next to the hinge, and was now walking aimlessly across the rear deck, having vague thoughts about bees and a fairy princess, when it suddenly flashed into her mind that she was she. Her movements froze, and she looked at herself, insofar as she was able to do so. She could not see much, except for the front of her skirt and her hands when she raised them to inspect them, but this was enough for her to get a general idea of the small body she suddenly realized was hers, . . . each idea was a short flash, quite innocent of words, her thoughts wandering sporadically, as she sometimes thought about nothing, followed by thoughts about the bees and the fairy princess. If you would add up the total of the moments of deliberate thought, you would maybe get to four or five seconds, spread out over the course of more than half an hour of nothing."[2]

Hughes was asked by the philosopher Herbert Spiegelberg whether his description of Emily was perhaps a childhood memory of himself. He answered that this was indeed the case. However, he had been younger than his 10-year-old Emily, aged 6 or 7 instead:

> "Oddly enough, when I wrote the book, I remembered that it happened just as casually to me as to Emily, but at this moment [35 years later DK], I wonder whether the experience was not triggered by another incident, the nearly unbearable scene of a cat playing with a mouse which was still alive. I identified with the desperate, tortured mouse, and the discovery that I was not that mouse could have led me to the question who I actually was. Both incidents are linked to the same bit of garden path in my memories, but I remember them separately and have no proof that they occurred simultaneously."

The fact that Emily's experience made an impression is also clear from the fact that not only Sartre, but also Erich Fromm[3] and Simone de Beauvoir[4] used it in their reflections.

In this situation, we have a novel writer who uses his own childhood memory as an event for one of his characters.

Another example is the Dutch-American author Dola de Jong in her novel *En de akker is de wereld.* In this memory, awareness of time plays a role again. Just like Hughes, Dola de Jong planted her own childhood memory in her character Maria. When I asked her, shortly before her death, whether she had experienced herself what she had ascribed in her novel to her main character Maria, she answered that the scene must without any doubt have come from her own childhood, though she could no longer call the episode to mind.

It happens during the war. Maria is in her early years of puberty and living temporarily with the Dutch consul and his family in Tanger, waiting for a boat to Lisbon to travel on to the United States:

Dola de Jong (1911–2003)

"That evening, before falling asleep, Maria heard the clock stop. The ticking of the clock had suddenly moved out of the silence, clearly and empathetically. A hasty ticking, suddenly interrupted, followed by silence, unfathomable, deep silence. She jolted up, the ticking of the clock inside her, vibrating throughout her body. But the room was filled with silence. I heard the clock stop, she thought, I, Maria, heard the clock stop. It was an immense event, the greatest. I, Maria Lefkowitz, heard the clock stop. She was sitting in the world, the black silence, the endless world. And then came the discovery. I am I. I, Maria Lefkowitz, am I. And back to the immense event, I heard the clock stop. I heard it! I! I, Maria Lefkowitz. I am sitting here. And outside is the world, endless, and I am I. And the surprise, the awe of the miracle, 'I'."[5]

The previously mentioned Frederik van Eeden also describes how a girl suddenly discovers her 'self' in his famous book *Van de koele meren des doods.* The 9- to 10-year old Hedwig, who later became psychotic:

Frederik van Eeden (1860–1932)

"However, she was in no way a sad child . . ., but she had, virtually unnoticed by anyone who knew her, brief periods of withdrawal, sometimes lasting a few minutes, during which it seemed like she was looking deep into herself in an incomprehensible and stifling manner. She would mumble her own name, 'Hedwig, Hedwig Marga de Fontayne, me, me, me, -, myself, I am Hedwig de Fontayne', and it would seem like she was staring into abysses which depth and unfathomability would take her breath away. These moments were rare, and she forgot none of them, nor the place, environment, and the position in which she experienced them. Among the large, white marble of the hallway, two were seemingly cut from one piece, with their separating edges facing up, which were placed such that the pattern of the veins made up a large and white heart of a giant. Kneeling before this in thought, as she had recently pointed it out to a friend as a unique characteristic of the house at an afternoon late that winter, Hedwig experienced her strongest sudden self-insight. And this time, it would serve as her type or archetype for all other times. She was clear-headed and happy the rest of the day, like someone who has a joyful secret hidden away from others."[6]

Another Dutch psychiatrist, H.C. Rümke, who analyzed Hedwig's case, wrote the following about this:

> "[This] is a very original observation which I had never encountered in psychopathological literature, not even in Pierre Janet, who is a master in representing experiences at the threshold of the normal and abnormal."[7]

But no, even though Hedwig became psychotic, I have now read enough descriptions of memories that make it likely that children can have such experiences and stay very healthy later in their youth and adulthood.

Besides the fact that authors sometimes attribute their own sudden flashes of self-awareness to children in their novels, a number of them spoke about these own experiences in their autobiographies. The oldest one I know of is by Jean Paul in his *Selberlebsbeschreibung*, published posthumously. Just like Jung, he was the son of a pastor and lived during his childhood in a parish in Bavaria. We do not know how old he was when the following happened to him, only that he was '*sehr junges Kind*':

Jean Paul (Johann Paul Friedrich Richter 1763–1825)

> "I will never forget the experience which I have not told anyone about until now, when I witnessed the birth of my self-awareness. I still clearly remember the time and the place. One morning, when I was still a very young child, I stood in the front-door, looking at a pile of wood to my left, when the sudden realization that 'I am an I' (ich bin ein Ich) hit me like a bolt of lightning from the sky and stuck

with me. And ever since it has remained with me luminously: at that moment my I (Ich) had seen itself for the first time, and forever. One can hardly think of a deception of memory in this case, since no one else's reporting could mix additions with such an occurrence, which happened merely in the curtained holy of holies of man and whose novelty alone had lent permanence to such everyday concomitants."[8]

From the south of Germany to the former Russia before the revolution, Vladimir Nabokov describes an event from when he was 4 years old in his autobiography *Speak, Memory*:

Vladimir Nabokov (1899–1977)

"Initially, I did not realize that time, which initially seems so unlimited, was a prison. When I dug around in my childhood (which is the second-best form of digging around, just behind digging around in your eternity, I consider the birth of self-awareness as a series of scattered flashes, which gaps gradually fade away until clear blocks of observation arise, affording memory a slippery hold.) I had learned to count and talk virtually simultaneously at a very young age, but the inner knowledge that I was I and that my parents were my parents seemed to only have established itself later, when these ideas were directly related to my realization of their age compared to mine. Based on the bright sunlight which immediately permeates my mind with round sun spots through overlapping leaf patterns when I think about this revelation, the event may have been my mother's birthday in the country in late summer, where I asked questions and considered the answers I received. This is all in line with the principles of the recapitulation theory: the start of the reflexive awareness in the brains of our earliest ancestor must have decisively coincided with the days of the awareness of time. This is why something happened to me when my recently revealed, fresh, and neat formula of my own age of four was confronted with the parental formulas of thirty-three and twenty-seven. I experienced a tremendous, enticing shock. . . . At that moment, I realized clearly that the twenty-seven-year-old creature wearing soft white and pink, holding my left hand was my mother, and that the thirty-three-year-old creature wearing hard white and gold, holding my right hand was my father. While they walked a steady pace, I tiptoed between them, sometimes jauntily, at other times at a trot, from sun spot to sun spot, in the middle of a path I can still easily recognize as a lane with tiny decorative oaks in the park of our Wyra estate in the former province of Sinter-Petersburg in Russia. In fact, I can see my paltry self celebrate the birth of conscious life on this August day in 1903 from my current position of superiority of remote, isolated, and virtually uninhabited time."[9]

Nabokov thought about a series of scattered flashes, not of merely one, like most people do. But the awareness that 'I was I, and my parents were my parents' is still a 'tremendous, enticing shock' after this series of flashes. Nabokov did not describe any recurrence of such shock in all of the pages of his childhood memories that follow. For him too, this single event must have been a unique case, which details have remained just as clear as for Richard Hughes. Particularly these associated memories of a specific situation in which the event occurred make me trust many of these descriptions and convince me that they have not sprouted from fantasy afterward. The same elements often reoccur in such memories. Such as the playful effect of the sunlight at a place the child is looking at.

I found another nice memory in which sunlight plays an important role. This memory is by the French scholar in literature Jacques Lusseyran, a blind resistance hero who survived Buchenwald. He turned blind when he was 8 years old. This made the memory of his fourth birthday he describes all the more special.

Jacques Lusseyran (1924–1971)

"I was always running during my childhood years. But I did not run to get to something, like adults do. I used to run to get a closer look at things I thought I could see in the distance. And also to see all the things I had not even thought of yet. I ran from place to place, like it was some kind of stage race.

And this is how I see myself running on my fourth birthday. . . . I ran across the pavement to a cross of light, made up by three streets, the Rue Edmond, the Rue Sedillot, and the Rue Dupont-des-Loges, where we lived. A triangle of sunlight, like you see when approaching the seafront, appeared in the direction of the Avenue Rapp. I was drawn into the great power of that concentration of light. Frantically waving my arms and legs, I shouted at myself: 'I am four years old and I am Jacques!'"[10]

A great number of memories people have shared with me contain a description of sunlight, not always as poetically as previously mentioned, but with conviction. An example: a girl is sitting on the toilet, and the sunlight hits her arm through the small window of the bathroom; she looks at the hairs on her arm, clearly visible in the sunlight, and she suddenly experiences the shock of awareness: I am!

Or a boy who was walking home in the former Dutch Indies and sees the sun shining on a new copper cent he had just received, and suddenly, the realization hits!

But sunlight is not a requirement, as the flash of self-awareness can also occur in the dark. Just think about what Dola de Jong described earlier.

The Dutch author and history scholar Jacques Presser also became suddenly aware of 'an I in myself'. He is 6 or 7 years old at the time and standing in the garden of his parental home in Antwerp:

Jacques Presser (1899–1970)

> "Strange, I can still see myself in that garden at a very specific moment, as if I had consciously wanted to capture a moment in time: I am standing on a square piece of wood and am calling out to my parents to come out and look at me: 'Look, I'm sailing a boat!' The strange thing is, I am still utterly certain that I did this, but also of the fact that I actually observed myself doing this, and that I suddenly became aware of an I in myself at that specific point in time."[11]

The young Jacques experienced a type of observing I, resulting in the observation of an acting I in himself. I encountered this duality again and again in numerous memories, described as 'I and me' or 'I and myself'.

I want to conclude with two childhood memories of modern authors.

This memory of the British novelist Ian McEwan is included in *Hockney's Alphabet*, a book by the British artist David Hockney, found under the title of Joy and the letter J:

Ian McEwan (1948)

> "We lived in Tripoli when I was nine years old. I had an experience of immense joy at that time, and even though it barely lasted thirty seconds, I regard this as the real start to my conscious life. I joined my mum on her way to work one early morning during the summer holidays. She dropped me off at the local beach, where I was going to spend some time by myself for a couple of hours. I had a packed lunch with me and some change so I could buy myself a drink.

It was probably around half past seven when I was stood at the top of a low cliff, near some wooden steps. The tranquility of the Mediterranean Sea – certainly a great deal cleaner and brighter than it is today – was inextricably linked to the sweet mild air and the sound of breaking waves. The white beach was deserted. It was there just for me. The space between myself and what I saw was full of glistening meaning. Wherever I looked: yesterday's footprints in the sand, a bulge in the rocks, the wooden handrail of the stairs underneath my hand, everything seemed overwhelmingly unique, etched in light, and somehow aware of itself, 'knowing' itself.

But at the same time, everything belonged together, and this unity seemed to say: 'Now you've seen us.' I felt myself dissolve into what I saw. I was no longer a son, or a school boy, or a cub. And yet I felt my individuality very intensely, as if it were the very first time. I was becoming someone. I mumbled something like 'I am I, or 'This is me'.

I sometimes find these terms still very usable. I do not remember anything about the rest of that day."[12]

The level of detail in the description of the surroundings is striking. I encountered this often in the memories people sent me. To me, this enhances the authenticity and believability of these memories.

Henning Mankell, the Swedish author of detective novels, including the world-renowned Wallander series, decided to write an autobiography when he learned he was suffering from an untreatable form of cancer. He named his book *Quicksand*:

Henning Mankell (1948–2015)

"In the midst of the chaos of my feelings which had taken hold of me when my stiff neck abruptly turned out to be cancer, I noticed I was increasingly thinking back to my youth. It took me a little while to figure out that my memory was trying to be of service to me, offering me a starting point for dealing with the disaster that was happening to me. I simply had to start somewhere, and the choice was down to me. I was becoming increasingly convinced that I should be looking for that starting point in my early life. I opted for a cold winter's day back in 1957. When I woke up that morning, I was still completely ignorant of the fact that a major secret would be revealed to me that day. I am walking to school at an early morning. I am nine years old.

> . . . I had an extraordinary experience that cold morning, fifty-seven years ago, which would affect the rest of my life. I can still remember this event very vividly. The memory is engraved in my mind. I was suddenly filled with inspiration. It was like a shock went right through my body. Words just started filling my head. 'I am I, and no one else. I am I.'
>
> At that moment, I become aware of myself. Before this I was merely a child with childish thoughts. But this was the start of a whole new phase. Awareness is essential to your own identity. I am I, and no one else. I am not interchangeable with someone else. Life had suddenly become serious. I am not sure how long I continued standing there in the cold and dark with this new, amazing insight. I only remember that I was late for school that day . . . I was never late, so Miss Prestjan only looked at me questioningly and then nodded. . . . I sat down at my desk and looked around. Nobody knew anything about this huge secret I have been carrying with me since that cold winter's morning in 1957."[13]

This chapter started with a quote by Sartre. I want to end in the same way. In response to Hughes's young protagonist Emily, Sartre wrote:

> **Jean-Paul Sartre (1905–1980)**
>
> "This flash of intuition is completely empty: the child had only just been convinced that she is not a random person, or she becomes a random person because of this conviction. She is different from others, which is true, but each of those others is different in turn. . . . What to do with a discovery which frightens us and offers nothing? Most people try to forget it as soon as possible. But the child that discovered itself in desperation, anger, and jealously will base its entire life on the fruitless pondering about its formal state of difference. 'You have banished me', it will tell its parents. 'You have banished me from the perfect unity I was part of, you have sentenced me to an isolated existence. . . . If you want to draw me in and make me yours again, this would no longer be possible, as I have become aware of myself in opposition to all others.' . . . And to its school peers and the street lads following it, it will say: 'I am someone else. Someone else than all of you obstructing me. You can follow my body, but not my state of difference.'"[14]

Sartre may be supported in this idea by a passage from the autobiography of the author Julien Green, who would have been around 5 years old at that time.

Julien Green (1900–1998)

> "I was sitting in front of the window when I suddenly became aware of my existence. Everyone has had this remarkable moment of being separated from the rest of the surrounding world. . . . That is when I left paradise. It was the melancholic moment at which the first person singular enters the human existence to stand at the front of the stage until his last breath of air . . . expelled from the Garden of Eden by the angel with the flickering sword who calls himself Me."[15]

Thinking about the memories of the authors in this chapter for whom the discovery of the self was nearly an ecstatic experience, I believe that Sartre adopted a quite one-sided interpretation of the limited number of descriptions of experiences in his possession. He was probably led astray by a memory of André Gide (André, 11 years old, and crying in his mother's lap: 'I am not like the others'.)[16] which I consider not very characteristic of the type of insights in which I am interested. The realization of being *different* from other children is something else than the realization of his own *individuality*.

It is true, I have received a couple of memories in which sudden self-awareness is accompanied by feelings of fear of being alone, and in which the negative mood of this memory prevails in later stages of life.

But I have many more memories in which the narrator remembers a moment of tense amazement, joy, and pride. The next chapters contain numerous examples of this. The statements by the narrators about their lives after their experience rarely refer to any negative lingering effects on their minds.

Notes

1 Jean-Paul Sartre (1947) *Baudelaire*. Literary Criticism.
2 Richard Hughes (1932) *A High Wind in Jamaica*. New York, Modern Library.
3 Erich Fromm (1941) *Escape from Freedom*. New York, Farrar & Rinehart.
4 Simone de Beauvoir (1948) *l'Existentialisme et la sagesse des nations*. Paris, Gallimard.
5 Dola de Jong (1945) *And the Field Is the World*. New York, Scribner's Sons.
6 Frederik van Eeden (1900) *Van de koele meren des doods*. Amsterdam, Versluys.
7 H.C. Rümke (1964) *Over Frederik van Eeden's Van de koele meren des doods: Essay*. Amsterdam, Scheltema Holkema.
8 Jean Paul (1883) *Selberlebensbeschreibung. Zweite Vorlesung Werke*. München, Carl Hanser Verlag.
9 Vladimir Nabokov (1951) *Speak, Memory*. London, Victor Gollancz.
10 Jacques Lusseyran (1999) *And There Was Light*. New York, Parola Books.

11 Jacques Presser (1985) *Louter verwachting*. Amsterdam, Arbeiderspers.
12 David Hockney (1991) *Hockney's Alphabet*. London, Faber & Faber.
13 Henning Mankell (2014) *Quicksand*. New York, Random House/Vintage.
14 Jean-Paul Sartre (1947) *Baudelaire*. Literary Criticism.
15 Julien Green (1963) *The Green Paradise*. New York, Barnes & Noble.
16 André Gide (1924) *Si le grain ne meurt*. Paris, Gallimard.

4

AWARENESS OF BEING

A friend of our family wrote an autobiography for her grandchildren on the occasion of her hundredth birthday. Her children turned this into a book and gave me a copy. In this book, I found a memory of back when she was 4 years old. She was living with her parents on the island of Ceram in the Dutch Indies.

She still remembered sitting on the veranda of her parental home with a view of the garden and the sea beyond it, 'surrounded by all my dolls and toys'. And suddenly she thought: 'How nicely I am sitting here'. ('Wat zit ik hier fijn'.) That moment and that single sentence became so engraved in her memory that she was able to include it in her autobiography when she was almost 100 years old.

A seemingly everyday phrase, 'I love sitting here', four words, thought up by a 4-year-old child, unmistakably refers to a sensation of herself, an awareness of being, and thus of self-awareness.

A Dutch publicist and translator described a similar experience, even though she was older than the narrator previously mentioned:

> "I was eight years old and on my way to the changing rooms in the swimming pool. I was just about to get my B diploma. I suddenly got a strong awareness of my presence, specifically there, at that time, and of the fact that I was I, and that I was eight years old".

'Had a strong awareness of my presence'. I propose to use here the phrase 'awareness of being' to make it clearer what we are talking about, even more so than when using the word 'self-awareness'. I thought it right to add 'awareness of being' to the concept of self-awareness. 'I am on my way to the changing rooms and I am eight years old'.

The next memory contains something similar. The author could no longer remember her precise age. But it was during her years attending primary school:

> "I was at the playground of the Nutsschool at the Laan van Poot in The Hague. We were playing around and I was facing the school wall. I assume I was counting down while playing hide and seek, or something similar. I had some time. Standing there, I became focused on the details of the wall, the seams, a bit of contamination or vegetation. That is when I experienced a great sense of identity. Something like 'I am this person, I am standing here, I am myself, I am the one looking, I see the world around me, and I am the one able to do so'. An enormous feeling of joy of 'me, alone'. This feeling has been with me since, I believe, at numerous times when I am alone. Which is not all that often because of a busy family life with four children and a busy job in secondary education."

'An enormous feeling of joy'. It is certainly not the case that all children are similarly happy with this sudden awareness of being. We have already seen this in the chapter on authors. There may be a fundamental difference in personality and character that determines who feels happy, free, in control, and who feels frightened and lonely in the face of such transcending insight – the feeling of joy of 'me, alone' in contrast with the fear of 'me, alone'.

The current parental bonding theory would consider the first response typical for a 'safe attachment relationship' with the parent(s), the second for an 'unsafe or anxious attachment relationship'. However, psychologists who specialize in personality believe that children can also be anxious or cheerful and fearless by nature, entirely unrelated to the relationship with their parents.

I would not consider this difference between happy and anxious in response to such experience overly important to the later development. It is unlikely to have any predictive worth. An example of how little negative feelings in response to such experience tell something about the future is provided by this young 24-year-old woman:

> "I was around nine or ten years old. It was at night and completely dark. I was lying in bed and had difficulties sleeping. As usual, I was probably thinking about the things that happened that day, but I

> am not sure exactly. Suddenly, out of nowhere, I had the realization that 'I am I; I am the only one in the world who is me'. I felt like this realization came out of nowhere and this frightened me a little. I felt trapped in my own body, and it felt quite lonely. This feeling lingered a bit, even though I kept thinking that night and realized that everyone is his or her own I. I am now used to this 'being me', but there are still times at which I suddenly realize this, and this can still amaze me. However, this is no longer associated with any negative feelings."

Out of nowhere. This was also the memory of a woman, now aged 51, from back when she was 7:

> "I remember everything very precisely. The weather and what I was wearing. I was walking to school because the lunch break was nearly over. There were already children playing and running in the school yard. I suspect that I was a dreamy child. That afternoon, at least, I was turned into myself, even though this phrase does not fully describe it. I was singing a song I had heard on the radio. I have always thought it was 'Let it be' by the Beatles – based on the realization that I knew that something like the Beatles existed. But I was not aware of that at the time. I walked into the schoolyard and nothing was wrong during my first two steps, but it suddenly dawned on me at step three: 'I am someone!' And the world became completely different at that moment. In my experience, at least. A quite essential 'different way of looking' at the world around me and at who I was."

The awareness of being: 'I am someone'. In many I-experiences, children are alone, but just like in this example, they can be among others, but still isolated in a certain sense. The shock experience may also occur while a child is part of a group. In the next memory of a 73-year-old woman, she was a child sitting at a table with a large group of people when she had what she calls a 'revelation':

> "I was around nine years old and sitting at the dining table with eleven others eating a warm meal at noon. These others were my father, mother, grandparents, a sister, four brothers, two store employees, and a maid. We had a store attached to our home, a textile shop opened during noon. Because customers kept arriving, the door opened and closed from time to time because one of the store

> employees went to the store and came back. The door had a spring at the top. While I was looking at this spring, a sudden flash pops into my mind, something like 'Hey, I am I, and they are also I's!'. That is quite remarkable!' I cannot remember the conversation at the table, but I do not think it matters, just like the spring did not matter. . . . I did not talk about this 'revelation' at the table; I think I would have hardly had the words to express myself at the time."

When someone remembers the sudden self-awareness in the company of others, it is of course possible that something in the conversation of or with those others has triggered the own thoughts. But since most experiences occur when a child is alone, one can assume that the meeting at the table in this example did not matter. A child can be turned into itself amidst others, just like adults. Just like in this memory of a young woman in her early 30s:

> "It was a morning in fifth grade. My best friend was in the hospital and people were afraid she would die. I was in Catholic school and prayed in class for the first time that day. I would never do this; we were not religious at home. There was a porcelain angel in our classroom, and I was looking at it. Class had already started. Suddenly, a deep feeling arose within me. I felt how it entered me layer by layer, and thought: 'I am I, I am Liesbeth; and this will never change.' It was also quite frightening, as this meant I would never be able to get rid of myself. But it was also beautiful, as I would experience all sorts of things and truly feel them. 'I was I'. When I repeated these words later, I felt this sensation of descending layer by layer again, even now. As a child, I could get lost in thought at times, and I never really spoke about this with my parents. I felt quite lonely at times, but I had myself from that moment on."

This '[entering] me layer by layer' is unique in my collection – the *observing I* that descends into the *existing I* step by step. The term 'introspection' is given an entirely physical meaning here. The I as observer descends, possibly from the frontal lobe of the cerebral cortex, into the older I, the I of the playing and experiencing child, while the child simultaneously realizes that this will be forever its home.

Which, naturally, is a sad fact. Many of us would be very happy to move their observing I to another mind or another body, as long as they could take their memories with them. But the relief of being home at yourself still prevails during childhood, as long as these are not unhappy years. Of course, whether the looming death of the friend and the corresponding disappearing I played a role in this case cannot be determined. But the threat of death, of yourself, your parents, your brothers and sisters, will certainly more often lead to a more intense awareness of being.

5

I AM I, AND NOT SOMEONE ELSE

When putting their memories into words, the persons writing the letters sometimes clearly indicate that their sudden self-awareness made them feel removed from others, whether or not they were physically present near them. A writer and publicist aged 48 noted:

> "I am seven years old. I left school a bit earlier. The teacher had sent me to my closest friend, Tilly. She lived a small distance away from the village in a farm among the pastures. She had stayed home today because she was not feeling well. I had often walked this road before, but never without Tilly. It is around 2 o'clock, and there is an oppressive heat and complete silence. A few birds are sitting on the barbed wire. The sandy road has deep cracks and I try not to trip over the rocks. My stockings have sagged, just like the suspenders of my green checkered skirt. The school is far behind me, a small dot on the horizon. Just as far before me I can see the low roof of Tilly's farm. I stand still to look at a plane leaving a line in the air. I track it with my finger. And that is when it happens. With all intensity, I realize that I am 'I'. Not my parents. Not Tilly. I. I exist. Here and now. I wake up in my own life, in which I am the protagonist. It is an overwhelming experience. I have passed a threshold. I abruptly come home in myself. How long I have been standing there on that sandy road below the burning sun with my new insight, I cannot remember. Nor how the rest of the afternoon went. I do know that I

> did not tell it to anyone. I had initially forgotten it but reading your book 'I am I' made me remember it again."

'I am not Tilly, not my parents'. They are the others. The child separates itself from those others. This is described beautifully by a middle-aged psychologist and publicist:

> "I was seven years old and staying at my grandmother's home for a few days. It was an enormous house. . . . I was staying there and remember wandering around the ground floor, from the dining room through the office to the conservatory, from the seating area to an extension with green velvet furniture nobody ever used, when I was suddenly struck by the thought 'I am I'. This is why this was so remarkable, because I immediately realized that this was the first time in my life I had thought that. It was like I had not existed before this moment. It was a moment of great clarity. I was no longer one with myself, but observed myself from up above, as it were. The realization that I was the only one who could think about myself as 'I' was new and strange.
>
> Afterwards, I was able to explain why this thought struck me right there and then. I was a shy child and had not stayed over anywhere before. No matter how nice everyone in my grandmother's home was to me, it was not like home. In your own home, everything is self-evident; your family members are almost an extension of yourself. When I was staying over, this mindless self-evidence disappeared. The distinction between myself and other people struck me intensely and I became aware of myself."

Looking at yourself 'from up above', as it were, is so common that I have written a separate chapter on it. But I have not often encountered this levelheaded and plausible explanation why the I-am-I experience occurred precisely at that time. The reason in this situation seems to be the interrupted symbiotic relationship with one's own household, where the 'family members are almost an extension of yourself'.

The following memory contains a hint of something similar. Not the familiarity of the parental home, but that of your old school. A young woman wrote that she was an introvert when she was a child and spoke little about her personal thoughts and feelings with the people around her, including her parents. She had the following experience when she was 13:

> "It happened in the first week of my first year in secondary school. I was home alone. I suddenly realized that I was a human, someone, a person, distinct from other people. It felt like I was a flower that suddenly bloomed, like the top of my skull opened up, like cool water flowed through me. I felt strong, happy, and filled with opportunities. . . . I believe that the transition to the new school triggered this sudden self-awareness."

The reason for this insight was the realization of a new life, away from, as she wrote, the strict primary school with a rigid educational program.

There are only a few men among the people who wrote me letters. Are women more prone to self-reflection? I have included three nice memories of men next. The first man was 8 years old when the following happened to him:

> "I was walking home around noon on a sunny road, probably from the post office on Semarang where my father worked as a sous-chef. I had received a beautiful, shiny, light-bronze cent from him, with a hole in the middle. This was normal in many coins in Asia, as this enabled them to be threaded on strings. It was completely new and packaged in a white piece of cardboard, wrapped in shiny clear film. The cent reflected the bright light. It was engraved with '1937'. This struck me and ingrained this memory forever. I suddenly realized that I was I, and not someone else, and that I was living now, in 1937, here and now. I continued home at a fast pace, somewhat bewildered."

As I wrote previously, sunlight plays a role in many memories, and I have dedicated a separate chapter to it as a result.

Years and ages, changing from year to year, are common triggers as well. The realization of one's own individuality, living 'here and now', often coincides with a moment of focus on the 'lifetime' of a person.

The second memory is by a 68-year-old man:

> "I was around seven years old when it happened to me, in 1957 or 1958. And my recollection of this moment is still incredibly clear today (2018). It happened to me in the Kolensteegje ('Coal Alley') in Ede. . . . Just like every day, I walked through that alley on my way home from school on my own. It will have been very busy, like always. . . . I was walking through this crowd when, suddenly, in

> a flash, I realized that I was I and not one of the others around me or anywhere else. I also became aware of the fact that I was a type of center of the world for myself. It was just as much of a surprising experience as it was liberating. I continued staring down at the cobbles in the alley for a while in an attempt to process it all. It did not take me long to get home after that, and I would undoubtedly have returned to the exciting life of a seven-year-old boy again, but I still reflected on this special moment so often that I have never forgotten it."

The writer of the third example was 57 when he wrote me. He was around 9 years old when he had the following experience:

> "I was on my way back from school. I was walking on the right side of the road, which I can still remember clearly; whenever I think about this moment, I can immediately see the street in front of me. The thought was: 'How is it possible that I am I, and not someone else?' I still clearly remember the slight panic accompanying this thought. On the one hand because particularly the coincidence of this awareness has 'stuck' with me, and on the other hand because other people and the rest of the world seemed to depend on my awareness. However, the panic is mainly associated with the feeling that I was unable to grasp the situation in its entirety."

The same experience was quite frightening to one of my cousins:

> "I must have been around twelve or thirteen years old. I was in secondary school. Between lessons, students needed to move to a different classroom for the next lesson. The hallway would be filled with talking students walking in various directions. I remember walking among this crowd with my school bag in my hand one day. Looking at all the other children around me, I suddenly thought: 'These are all I's walking there, everyone is one, including me.' I suddenly felt alone there, lonely. The feeling that I was separated from all others. It was strange, a bit frightening."

I am I, and they are also all I's, all tiny I's. Me and the others. The realization in which the observing I realizes that it is irrevocably connected with the existing and acting I. Leading to the logical consequence that you, as the observing I, cannot walk in the shoes of another person, cannot be another person. A psychologist remembers the following from back when he was 10 years old:

> "I was walking in the Utrecht city center with my parents, close to the station, in the weekend. It was quite a sunny day and there was little traffic. I hated these weekend walks and was usually trailing well behind my parents. A cyclist rode towards us from the opposite direction. The footpath was a meter or so higher than the cycling path at that spot. I was suddenly overwhelmed by the following realization: 'Why am I I, and why am I not that cyclist?' I may have briefly panicked because of the thought that my I could transfer to this cyclist, but at the same time, I felt connected to my body walking there with all kinds of ties. However, I believe that I was suddenly overwhelmed by anxiety for a brief period. I have never experienced the same intensity afterwards. Nor have I told my parents, sister, or friends about the event."

In some of the I-am or I-am-I experiences, one's own name plays an important role. You can imagine this being self-evident, as a child knows which name belongs to him or her from an early age. Moreover, a child will usually have realized this at such a young age that he or she has become aware of this bit by bit, sometimes leading to a sudden realization in slightly older children (as in the case of Jacques Lusseyran 'I am Jacques!'). A young woman writes:

> "I believe that I must have been between six and eight years old when I was standing in the kitchen watching my mother prepare dinner. At some point, I became enticed by continuously repeating my name. I cannot remember whether I did this out loud or in my mind, but I suspect that it was the latter. 'Froukje, Froukje, Froukje' . . . and so on. This is when I was struck by the feeling that this name was mine, and that I was I. The feeling that it was actually very special that I existed. It was like I became a bit separated from myself. A type of clarity or amazement. I compare it to something like 3D drawings: you can suddenly see another dimension. This overwhelmed me so much that I immediately told my mother. However, she did not really understand what I meant, also because I was unable to explain it properly."

I am Froukje, and nobody else is Froukje. One's own name and mother also play a role in the following memory:

> "I was attending the Nieuwe Lyceum in Hilversum in the third year of the Higher Civic School. I was thirteen. We were played the *Erlkönig* during a lesson taught by our music teacher. *Wer reitet so spät durch Nacht und Wind, es ist der Vater mit seinem Kind.* The risk of the imposing death of the boy could be felt in the threatening tone. The voice of death, however, is enticing and flattering. The music really struck me; I had never experienced such an overwhelming emotion before. I drowned in feelings. I came home and told my mother what had happened to me, and told her: 'How strange, I only realize that I exist now, that I *am* Helly, and am not merely *called* that.' Later, she 'randomly' gave me a gift: Der *Erlkönig* on a single."

A child who could share her experience with her mother, and a mother who demonstrates her understanding in a subtle way. This is something every child would wish for.

You cannot be somebody else, cannot step into someone else's shoes, but you can understand another, empathize with another. Children can also suddenly have this realization.

This will be discussed in the following chapter.

6

I CAN SOMETIMES PUT MYSELF IN SOMEONE ELSE'S SHOES

Numerous studies in the field of developmental psychology have been dedicated to 'role taking' or 'perspective taking': the ability to put yourself in someone else's shoes when someone has a different view on or different knowledge about things than yourself.

The gradual development of this mental capacity in children is an important theme in developmental psychology. Conflicts (of interest) presumably play an important role in this respect.

The ability to understand the thoughts and emotions of another person is supported significantly by language development.

There are many debates about the question whether some animal species can understand the thoughts and feelings of other animals and people. People who are very fond of their pet often think that this is the case. Movies about altruistic dogs and dolphins also suggest this. Many animals in books and movies for children are just as able to understand the thoughts and feelings of others as human children, with varying levels of success. But how many of these seemingly intelligent social actions of animals are solely the result of conditioning? There is a suspicion that psychopathic criminals can commit their crimes in cold blood because they have insufficiently learned to understand the thoughts and feelings of others.

Among the memories of sudden flashes of insight people have sent me, various examples contain a sudden realization of living in a prison of subjectivity. This is accompanied by the conclusion that everyone has this handicap. This is often the start of a *deliberate* attempt to look at the world through the perspective of another person.

When a child suddenly realizes this – as some children have this sudden insight – it has already shown gradual signs of being able to understand the thoughts and feelings of others for years. However, it was not aware of the fact that it was doing this! Just like we all are not always *aware* of everything during our daily lives.

Group play during school breaks seems to be a good situation for such insights to come to the surface, at least among girls, as I have not received any memories from men who remember playing in the schoolyard when they were still boys. Various memories in my collection are linked to a schoolyard or its immediate surroundings. I will give three examples.

The first example is provided by an 87-year-old woman. She starts her story with an I-am-I experience that will by now be familiar to the reader. This is followed by her insight into the relativity of subjective observation:

> "I was seven years old and was standing with my back to the schoolyard to cross the road when I suddenly realized: 'How strange to be here.' I have another memory of standing there from this same period, but this time I faced the schoolyard together with a friend. Kids were playing tag. For some reason, a red sweater one of the kids was wearing caught our attention. I said: 'Red can be something entirely different for me than for you.' 'What do you mean?' she said, 'isn't red, red?' I answered: 'We both use the word red, but I can never look through your eyes, and you cannot look through mine.' She called me 'weird' and walked away."

The second example is from a young 23-year-old Dutch woman when aged 7 or 8 and in the second grade of primary school:

> "I walked onto the schoolyard, as school was yet to start. I was still some distance away from the playground and was looking at kids playing around. I was looking at a classmate, a girl, and saw her run around and play. They were probably playing tag. That is when I thought: 'I am I, I am myself, I cannot switch with her and be her. I cannot switch with anyone else. I will always be Hanneke.' I also thought about the other children I saw playing around: 'They, too, cannot switch with others, and are all themselves.' I also thought something about how those children did not know I was thinking this. I was looking at them from both a literal distance and from a

distance in my mind. This gave me a strange feeling. I have no other memories about this, I can only remember what I thought. Before and after this moment, I felt like I was not completely present; I was unable to pay attention to many things around me. It took a year, until in the third grade, that I became fully present again."

Both cases start with the I-am-I thought, followed by the realization that the child can only look through his or her own eyes, an awareness of a distance between himself or herself and others, which seems to be irreconcilable. However, the realization that you are able to understand the thoughts and feelings of others can also arise at an early age as well as the fact that individuals can have relationships and friendships. I received the following example from a Dutch language expert and publicist:

"It must have been in the fourth grade when I was nine years old, when I suddenly became aware of being someone else than my friend I spent every day with. It was during the morning break, and we were playing hopscotch on a track we had drawn ourselves with another girl, on a quiet path around the school. We were playing behind our own classroom, out of sight, and away from the bustle of the schoolyard. My friend would have lunch with the girl we were playing hopscotch with. While I was watching my friend play, I suddenly lost interest in the game. I still remember precisely where I was standing on the side of the track. It seemed like I was floating away and ended up in another world.

That is when I realized that the girl playing hopscotch was my friend, and I was hers, and I wondered whether the other girl was also her friend, and whether this girl was my friend as well. I simultaneously realized that all three of us were different, separate individuals. (I probably did not yet know the word 'individual', but it does reflect what I became aware of at that moment).

I can also still remember wondering what the word friendship meant. I wanted to know why I liked her, and why she liked me. Back in the classroom, my schoolwork demanded my attention. But when I was walking back home during lunch break, I kept pondering these questions and frantically tried to determine how one could actually determine you were each other's friends."

The sensation of mentally moving away from the group game was experienced as 'floating away'. Those other girls will undoubtedly not have noticed this. They calmly continued playing hopscotch, while the author of this memory became aware of her place in the social network of her friends for the first time.

A great example of what is called 'perspective taking' in psychological literature.

Children who are friends frequently have fights. The girl in the following example is a few years older than the girl in the previous example, and the described memory is the result of a fight with a friend. The way thinking about the I-related subjectivity can lead to the proud realization of being a unique creature is shown in all its simplicity here:

> "I was in primary school and had a best friend with whom I used to do everything. We had a fight at some point. I was around eleven years old I believe. The anger had resided after some time and we were playing again. I can clearly remember playing outside together and on how I reflected on our fight. I suddenly realized that she had experienced our fight in an entirely different manner than I had. I literally thought: 'When I look through my eyes, I see things entirely differently than she does.' I realized for the first time that I could not see my own face when I looked around me. And that I saw the world from my perspective. This meant that somebody else, such as my friend, saw an entirely different world. And that when we were doing something, she would see an entirely different thing than I did. This insight made a strong impression on me. At that moment, it seemed like time and the world stood still. During the weeks that followed, and even in later years, I often looked at people while on my bike with the realization that they saw an entirely different thing than me. I realized that they saw a girl on a bike which would move from their field of vision in a few moments, without knowing who that girl was. It boils down to the following idea: 'They see me, I am part of their world, but they do not know me.' From this moment on, I gained the ability to see myself through the eyes of others, I became an individual to myself.
>
> Since the event made a deep impression on me, I have tried to explain it to others. Unfortunately, I was not often successful. Nobody shared my enormous enthusiasm about the discovery. I hope that you will understand what I am talking about."

This is a recurring experience: others failing to understand why the I-am-I realization has so much personal meaning. Those others cannot see the extraordinary in the ordinary. The obvious truth cannot invoke any emotions or sympathy in them. Just like a museum curator who cannot understand why a specific painting conjures up a tear in the eyes of someone looking at it. Or like the fisherman who cannot understand why people are looking at the sunset from a dike.

Our ability to understand the thoughts and feelings of others is limited. The familiarity with our common daily experiences in particular makes it more difficult to notice the unique or emotional aspects of this daily life experienced by others. The old, varied facades of buildings in a beautiful, historic city center are par for the course to persons living there. They can see tourists walk past in awe and take pictures. That is when they realize that these tourists are seeing something special in what is a regular occurrence to them.

I have included a few more examples of the sudden realization of the relative truth of one's own experience of reality next. Others are apparently experiencing something that is entirely different, even if you live in the same home with them or look at the same things. A young woman was 6 or 7 years old when she experienced the following:

> "I was sitting in the car with my father, mother, and sister. We had visited my grandmother and probably talked with her about the fact that another cousin had been born in the family. I was wondering where all these children were coming from, and when I asked my mother, she told me she would explain it to me back home. Apparently, she believed that my sister was still too young for these matters. Back home, my mother explained how things worked in a clear manner, and I was quite impressed. It was a strange idea that my parents were doing these sorts of things with each other. My parents were experiencing things I knew nothing about, things I did not even know existed until that day. This meant that everyone was experiencing different things and living different lives. A bit later, I realized that animals were also living different lives than people, and that the life of each animal was different in turn."

This woman, a medical analyst, added the following thought to this, which beautifully shows that there is a time for childlike amazement and the tendency to have introspective thoughts about things. It also shows that you can start asking questions when you grow older that cannot be answered. Thinking about these topics is postponed or given up entirely. After all, daily life demands enough attention:

> "Several insights followed, but I often felt like these matters were so difficult that I failed to reach a conclusion. I decided to no longer

> think about them after a while. And that is still the case now that I have become an adult."

Thoughts about the subjectivity of one's own experience can have such an impression on someone that he or she will start to wonder whether the things he or she is experiencing are real and not a dream. Entire philosophies are based on this idea, and many adolescents in particular explore this thought. It is very striking that even a 5-year-old kid can have similar ideas. A 45-year-old woman wrote me that this memory popped up when she was reading an article about this topic by my hand. She also wrote that she had never talked about this experience with anyone. She was 5 years old at the time:

> "I was playing outside with my friends. We were living in a flat above the stores on the fourth floor. My mother was home. I knew that my mother was keeping an eye on us from up above, which made me feel safe. I was playing downstairs on a wide sidewalk. It was cold, because I remember wearing a jacket and the fact that there was wind. My hair was blowing around my head. Even though I have forgotten their names, I also remember the faces of the children I was playing with. I was playing at the corner of the flat building, which housed a radio store. I was playing in the middle of the sidewalk, not below the large, wide canopy, as I could freely look into the street. The wind was blowing around the flat, and I suddenly realized that I was potentially the only one who was seeing everything. That there was no 'behind', only 'in front'. And that the world would turn with me if I turned my head. This thought startled me because I thought that my mother was possibly not real, just like my friends, the homes, the trees, the street, and the sky. That 'I' (but who was I?) was the only one who could see everything and that there were no others: I had made them up, and the space behind me was dark and empty. I stood still in the middle of the sidewalk and looked around me. The idea that I was potentially the only one who could see everything was frightening. Did everyone really exist? Were things real, or not real? I looked at my arms and moved them. I touched my sleeves with my arms, felt them, and looked whether they were really attached to my body. I also touched my friends and tugged on their coats. I also looked up quickly, because I thought that I should be able to get a glance of the darkness and emptiness if I had imagined my mother and looked

> up quick enough. When I later walked up the stairs back home and saw my mother, I had to touch her for a moment to check whether she was real. Fortunately, everything was 'real', but I really had to convince myself time and time again by touching everything. Even when the light was turned on in the evening and I saw and heard my father and mother at the dinner table, I remained wary. I had been in another country for a moment, where I was the only one, in which I very well may have imagined reality."

Another example, this time by a child who was a lot older, was submitted by a man in his 70s. The scene he describes is very touching, particularly in the context of the quotes at the end of this chapter from Anne Frank's diary. Anne has also stood on this platform.

> "I would have been twelve when I was staying in Amsterdam for a few days with my older sister working for a 'posh' family. We returned to Zeist together. The Amsterdam train station was the location from where one of the first deportations of the Dutch Jewish population took place. You were not allowed to go part of the platform. The mood was ominous. An old woman walked over to a soldier. I think she wanted to visit the restroom. The soldier gave her a strong shove with the butt of his gun. She fell. Both the soldier and me were looking at this old woman. That is when the following thought popped into my mind: 'Both me and the soldier are looking at the same thing, but we are seeing something entirely different. I am looking at a woman who could have been my grandmother. He is seeing an object. How is this possible?' I wondered whether knowledge is actually possible for the rest of my life. Is there something like true or good knowledge? It made me distrustful of philosophies that pretend to know what reality is like."

This boy momentarily stepped into the mind of the soldier and was shocked by the difference between his own observations and emotions and those of the soldier. These experienced differences later resulted in his relativistic ideas about true knowledge.

The capability to understand the thoughts of another person can also lead to sudden insights into the nature of your own personality, to a deliberate choice to start acting differently because you predominantly want to be 'grown-up' and want to start belonging to the world of adults. I want to start with an example of an 11-year-old girl, which she wrote down when she was 40:

> "I was in the fifth grade and walking arm-in-arm with a group of girls on a wide sidewalk in front of the school. It was a close group of girls talking about all sorts of things. I remember the topics of 'lesbian women' (very remarkable for a strict Christian school in the sixties), 'how to walk: with small or large steps, moving your hips or keeping taut', and 'stealing apples from the greengrocer'. My sudden realization occurred while talking and walking arm-in-arm. I suddenly realized that my dolls were dolls, and my game a game. I felt strange, like I was no longer myself, while simultaneously being more 'me'. And I suddenly knew that I would belong to the 'older ones', the older children of our family. I remember thinking: 'My childhood is over now'. Immediately followed by: 'But what if I play that I am playing?' But something had suddenly been overturned completely. I suddenly saw myself playing. It would never be the same again. The miracle was over. Unfortunately, I cannot remember what the others were talking about when this happened."

Other insights concern the role the *I* plays in the lives of others. I want to continue with two examples experienced by 13-year-old girls as sent to me by two young women, the first Dutch, the second Flemish:

> "I had gone swimming with some classmates at the Rijnvoorde pool in The Hague. It was during winter, and I was wearing a hat and gloves. There was a cold wind. After I had grabbed my bike, I suddenly realized that I was always being the clown, acting like the joker of the group, because I believed that others liked this. I suddenly became aware of the fact that I did not know who my true friends were. They liked me in my role of clown, but they could not see the true me. I decided to stop with this role on the spot. And I never picked it up again."

And

> "I was reading in a chair at my grandmother's house, while my nine-year-old cousin was sitting in another chair. We were being lazy and doing nothing all day, because I felt she was only a child. I suddenly realized how she must have been feeling, that I was doing the same

to her as older cousins did to me, and how unpleasant that was. That was the moment at which I started – with some difficulties at first – to treat her as an older girl by talking and laughing with her, which changed everything."

This shows how a sudden realization that you can step into someone else's shoes can lead to deliberate altruistic behavior almost immediately. The Flemish girl comes to this insight through analogous reasoning: what I am doing to her, others are doing to me. This girl was able to notice this similarity, thanks to the fact that she momentarily stepped into the mind of her younger cousin. Of course, this cousin did not understand the reason for the new cordiality. Does this simple memory not contain the essence of what people try to achieve through relationship and family therapy?

Let us return to the first memory in this chapter. In this memory, the I-am-I conclusion is followed by the realization of the inability to step into someone else's shoes. We have already seen examples of this in this book. Should the I-am-I experience not be seen as a step in the development of social thinking? Not of social acting, because this comes well before social thinking.

Focusing on the distinctiveness of one's own person is accompanied by the realization of the distinctiveness of the other. The *observing I* that steps away from its foundations and looks at one's own *acting I* suddenly also sees the other as a unique person from this position.

This stepping away from yourself is a change in perspective in itself. The child is looking at himself or herself in his or her mind. He or she becomes aware of his or her distinctiveness and accordingly of the distinctiveness of another child he or she spends a lot of time with. This realization gradually or suddenly expands to 'all others'.

This is later followed by the realization of knowing the other by stepping into his or her shoes. Afterward, or even simultaneously, a child will start noticing his or her characteristics, the roles he or she can have, based on the social environment he or she is in. The child learns to think about his or her own nature in certain conditions, such as when he or she is fatigued, forced, or competing with others. An example is the 15-year-old Anne Frank, who wrote the following in her diary on Saturday, July 15, 1944:

"I have a very visible trait which everyone who knows me for some time surely knows about, which is my self-knowledge. I can look at myself as if I were a stranger in all my actions. I face the everyday

> Anne without any presumptions or a bag of excuses, and watch what she is doing well or poorly. This same self-awareness never lets me go, and with each word I speak, I immediately know afterwards whether I should have said something differently or whether it is fine as it is."[1]

Four months earlier, on March 7, 1944, she looked back on how she was during her school years, before she went into hiding:

> "How did they see me at school? The one making jokes, always the first in line, and never in a bad or poor mood. Was it a miracle that everyone liked to ride their bikes with me or do a favor for me? I look down on this Anne as if she were a fun, but very shallow girl, who no longer has anything to do with me."

Two weeks later, on the first of August, she wrote the following in her diary to her imaginary friend Kitty:

> "I have told you more than once that my soul is split into two, as it were. The one side houses my expressive joy, my tendency to mock everything, my zest for life, and particularly the ability to see the bright side in everything. This includes my dislike of flirting, a kiss, a hug, an improper joke. This side is often lurking around and pushes away the other side, which is so much more beautiful, purer, and deeper. Nobody knows this beautiful side of Anne, which is why so few people can stand me. For sure, I am an amusing clown for one afternoon, after which everyone has had enough of me for a month. . . . You cannot imagine how often I have tried to hit, hide, or push away this Anne, which is only half of everything that is called Anne, but I cannot, and do not know why not."

I consider these impressive examples of how self-awareness can transition into self-knowledge during adolescence. This is the difficult stage to which attempts to change a personal perspective can lead, at least, when thought about and among introspective people. Not only are they now well able to understand the thoughts and feelings of others, but one's own person can now also be analyzed from various perspectives.

This leads to the hypothesis that the *I-am experiences* and the *I-am-not-the-other experiences* mark the start of a long road to the final stage of *'self-knowledge'* – experiences that only lead to such a leap in awareness in some that they are noticed and remembered. This awareness arises gradually among all others and is later considered so self-evident that people fail to see its uniqueness.

This is why I am afraid that by writing about it, I turn the phenomenon of the sudden I-am-I experience into something 'ordinary', due to which the fascination for the miracle of the leap in the childish mind may disappear. I also had to overcome the unwillingness to subject so many beautiful memories, which are all unique and valuable to the persons cherishing them, to rational categorization and analysis. Will this not tarnish their beauty?

I am reminded of a memory of an aunt of mine, then aged over 90, about what she experienced when she was sitting at a table with Fröbel weaving mats in front of her in Amsterdam, now nearly a century ago:

> "I cannot have been older than five. I was sitting at the table in the children's room of our home on the Nieuwe Keizersgracht. It was a round wooden table. My mother and the nurse would always sit there to sew. I can still see the holes of the tiny cog in front of me. I am sitting there to braid mats. All those shiny strips of paper in beautiful colors are lying in front of me. I cannot get enough of looking at them. I need to grab a few to be able to braid my mat, but I cannot. I cannot choose, everything is too beautiful. My mother is standing just off to the side of me, just like you are sitting there. She said: 'Do you not want to weave a mat? You have to choose now. If you do not make a choice, you cannot create a mat. And this will remain the case for your entire life. If you fail to choose now, you will never be able to.' And I became angry, truly angry. But intensely sad at the same time. I knew that she was right. I had to choose. But I also experienced this as an intense loss. This feeling of being lost in the colorful splendor could not persist. It was a moment of awareness. It was a separation between me and the things around me."

While writing this book, I encountered the need for more psychological organization and explanations of the childhood memories I collected. I had to start weaving mats.

Note

1 *De dagboeken van Anne Frank*, vierde verbeterende druk (1990) Amsterdam, Nederlands Instituut voor Oorlogsdocumentatie.

7

LIKE I WAS LOOKING AT MYSELF FROM THE OUTSIDE

Some people remember a moment on which they became aware of looking at themselves from a distance, without the link with a form of self-awareness or the question which *I* is being observed. For example, in the fragment of a memory from Chapter 5:

> "I was no longer one with myself, but observed myself from up above, as it were."

The following letter does not contain an observation 'from up above', but 'from a distance'. The author is a 75-year-old man, born in Surabaya, but who moved to the Netherlands during his childhood:

> "I would have been around eleven years old when I, presumably playing on the streets, momentarily leaning against a wall, had the experience or feeling of moving away from my location and looking at myself leaning against that wall from a distance. It could only have been a short time, during which I had a few thoughts, but I remember those as an experience of a kind I never had before."

Another man of about the same age wrote:

> "I was seven years old and lived in Rotterdam, near the river Maas. It was a bright, sunny day, and it was pleasant near the water. This was a popular area for boys like me to copy the older boys, fish up

> all types of things from the dirty Maaswater, such as bananas, peanuts, and sometimes even a coconut. . . . That day, I was alone at the water's edge. I was afraid of getting too close to the water without other boys from the neighborhood around. Rather than attentively investigating the water's edge for loot, I looked beyond it and saw the bustling port for the first time. It was a sensation of enormous spaciousness. At the same time, I experienced and underwent an 'out-of-body experience'. I saw myself standing from a distance and at a height of a few meters, and heard a voice say: 'You will always keep looking'. It was an entirely quiet moment, not at all frightening. I have never understood that voice and that out-of-body experience."

We move from these two older gentlemen to a young 21-year-old woman:

> "I would have been between ten and twelve years old. It was fall, early evening. It was already dark, raining, and there were strong winds. For reasons now unknown to me, I had walked into the garden and taken off my clothes at the back of the garden near the edge of the canal to become one with the wind and rain. I can only remember the following about the moment that I was standing there: it was like I was looking at myself from the outside. I can still remember every detail of this in that manner. I told my older sister that evening, but she looked at me like I was crazy."

Some readers may be thinking about the emerging sexuality at the start of puberty in this context. This will surely have played a role, but this explanation does not seem significant to me. At least not for the topic of this chapter: turning your own physical appearance into the object of your observation.

I consider looking at yourself, your *I*, from the outside as a moment at which the mind sees the entirety of your own body and forms an opinion about it without the help of a mirror.

Sexuality is more clearly present in the next description of a girl who was the same age at that time but is now a woman of middle age. The trigger seems to be the sudden realization of nudity. Even though this is only the case in the eyes of others, it switches to a top-down look at yourself to see yourself standing there, as it were. This girl was not alone, but in the presence of her entire family:

> "I believe that I was around ten or eleven years old. It must have been a Saturday afternoon, because that was the day on which we would all take a bath. This was a weekly recurring ritual. Two bathtubs

> would be placed in the living room and filled with warm water. A large tub for the three older children, and a small tub for the three younger ones. The baby would take a separate bath each day. I was lucky to be the oldest child because I was always the first to go into the clean water. The bathwater would not be refreshed for the other two, but only brought back to temperature with a bit of warm water. My mother would bathe the younger children and my father the older ones. It was always very cozy and pleasant, that bathing family. Until this Saturday afternoon. My father has given me a bath and I was standing in the tub to be dried off. And I suddenly saw myself standing there, in that tub, in the middle of the room filled with naked and half-naked brothers and sisters. I was no longer part of this scene but had stepped out of it as it were. Like a figurine in front of a backdrop. I experienced the feeling of nakedness for the first time. I cannot remember any details about this nakedness itself. I can only see a vague female body, which I looked down on from up above. 'I no longer want to take a bath with all of us', I said. My father's eyes told me that he understood. He helped me get down to the floor and gave me a towel so that I could dry myself off. This is where my memory ends. When I look back on this, I believe that this is the moment when I realized that I had a body and that this was something intimate, something you cannot simply show to everyone. I cannot remember whether this realization led to other changes in my actions. But this experience is still clearly engraved in my mind."

The observing *I* becomes detached from the acting and experiencing *I*, absorbed in the warm sensation of a family, a safe harbor, for the first time. This detachment is so specific in the experience that the child can see itself standing there from a position up above.

The following experience is by a man, a historic educationalist, who conducted many studies into Dutch autobiographical childhood memories recorded in the nineteenth and twentieth centuries. As a scientist, he is aware of the risk of misremembering early experiences.

> "It must have happened when I was between eight and eleven. I was alone in the lounge of our parental home and thinking about why I was the person I was. I did so by trying hard to see myself through the eyes of someone else. I believe through Tinie, the maid. Because I sort of resented her, this attempt had some importance for me, because I tried to adopt the perspective of someone I experienced as hostile. I remember that I thought it was easier to look at myself

through the eyes of my mother or a friend, as if this were a natural thing.

I was sitting on the corduroy sofa of my father. There was an old electric clock on the corner of the mantelpiece, which made a loud buzzing noise, which made me very aware of the time. I was startled, but also interested in suddenly seeing myself sitting on this sofa, approximately from the chandelier that hung in the middle of the high room. Being looked at from the outside had suddenly turned into something different than being seen through the eyes of another person, as this chandelier was significantly higher than any tall person. It was a somewhat scary experience, but I also felt very special. I tried to repeat it, but was unable to do so, or rather, it no longer touched me, it was no longer like looking from myself to the outside, which it felt like the first time. It had become like I was pretending it."

This is the only memory in my collection in which a child tries to repeat a random, spontaneously occurring self-observation. The realization of this boy that he was unable to do so, no matter how eager he was, has great significance. It enhances the probability of the truly undesired, nondeliberate childhood 'out-of-body experiences'. But this has not made them easier to understand. On the contrary. Another important aspect of this memory is that the boy had previously practiced looking at himself through the eyes of another person, exploring the image of himself. This is a nice expansion of what we have discussed in the previous chapter. The boy was already familiar with the thought-experiment of deliberately stepping into the shoes of an observer, to look at himself through the eyes of another person, at least at his appearance and his behavior as seen by others. Nevertheless, the observation from the chandelier, impersonal, struck him. Can this phenomenon be compared to what happens in dreams, fully autonomously – as in, not controlled by yourself – the creation of a story in which the I plays a variety of possible and impossible roles? If this is the case, it could be a form of daydreaming.

In Jung's memory of his I-am-I experience, the walking boy does not look at himself from a height or a distance. But he does experience himself as stepping out from the background: *'aus einem dichten Nebel herausgetreten zu sein'*.

This feeling of stepping forward is sometimes even accompanied by what feels like a great movement. A 76-year-old psychologist describes such a memory in the following example:

"I was fourteen years old. It was a warm summer day and I was pushing a stroller in which my youngest sister was sleeping. I was feeling very happy. I remember the dress I was wearing, which was my

> favorite dress, and the fun prospect of visiting the city center. It was the year of the Olympic Games (Berlin 1936) and the city was filled with strangers. All those languages I was hearing, but especially the many people with a dark skin, made me happy. Because I have a dark skin as well. There were only few people with a dark skin in Berlin at that time, and I had often heard that I was actually a stranger who did not match the ideal of 'the pure German people'.
>
> This was my mood when two ladies walked past me. I heard one of them say to the other: 'Look at that beautiful girl', and the other agreed. And I thought: 'They are talking about me, I am a person.' At the same time, I felt like I was being physically pushed forwards. It was like I were part of the background the one moment and was suddenly standing in front of it the next, as an independent person, three-dimensional. It seemed like I had the sudden insight that I could be seen and judged as a person.
>
> It is difficult to describe this experience, to find the right words for it, but I had certainly a clear feeling of looking at the world differently."

This psychologist linked her memory to the following observation:

> "I had heard that I was beautiful before, and I liked this, but this was something completely different. I suspect that the words of the ladies acted like a catalyst for something that was dormant within me. It is also interesting that I started seeing people differently from that moment. The social world I was living in had turned three-dimensional when I did. I am now seventy-six years old. Even though sixty-two years have passed, I feel like it happened yesterday. It made an enormous impact on me at that time. I have had multiple extraordinary experiences and religious experiences in my later life. If I compare these to this experience, I must conclude that the sensation of 'looking at the world differently' was the same in all of them. The major difference is that this was the first time I felt like an individual."

Bright awake in the middle of the day, walking along a lane or in a park, pushing a stroller. This girl was not alone and was aware of her surroundings. The psychologist suspects that this sudden awareness of her personality – to use that phrase – was dormant within her and that the remark acted as a catalyst. The disappearance of the fog had been prepared, and a suitable gust could suddenly blow it away. The girl suddenly sees herself as a person, as an individual. It feels itself separate from a background – with force, in this case – as if she were pushed forward.

An important theme in *Gestaltpsychology* is that sudden restructuring may take place in the way people look at the world when previously observed elements or even overall compositions of elements that follow autonomous rules of perception suddenly adopt an entirely new 'appearance'. Is this not just like what is described in this experience?

8

THIS IS MY BODY, I AM ALIVE!

The previous chapter contains two memories in which the own body is discovered, as it were. The experience of one's own body or body parts also has a central role in the sudden experience of individualization set out in other memories. A 72-year-old woman wrote the following about this:

> "I remember precisely where and when I discovered that I was **I**. I was changing clothes behind a chair. That is how we did it back in 1934. I suddenly 'saw' my own body with arms and legs. 'Those are mine. That is me, ME, ME. I want to never forget this', I thought. This gave me a strange feeling. I was looking at my mother and thought: 'And she also has an I, her own I. But I am eight years old and I can still enjoy playing. But when I am eight twice, I no longer can.' This seemed like a terrible thing to me."

This girl was not alone, and there was no special trigger. It was a day like any other, and she was doing a routine action, the daily act of getting dressed. The realization of 'this is my body' made her happy, as is the case in the other experiences discussed in this chapter. Only the realization of the transitionary nature of her age cast a shadow. 'I will no longer be able to play when I am sixteen'.

It was during the worldwide economic crisis, and children were growing up in a different world than they are now. Sixteen-year-old children would not have been playing in their social class. Which Dutch 8-year-old

could have this same thought now? Fortunately, this girl ended up well: 'I am now nine times eight years old, and I am playing again'.

We have already encountered the realization of one's own age compared to that of the parents in Vladimir Nabokov's memory.

The moment of awareness and the accompanying distancing from one's own body can also occur later, as described in the memories of a 44-year-old woman when she wrote a letter to me about a moment from back when she was 12:

> "It had been a hot day. I was walking to a nearby park after a great thunderstorm. It was almost dark while I was walking through the wet grass with bare feet. I suddenly look at my arms and legs and realize: 'Those are mine! This body is mine, I can do what I want with it. This life is my life, I will determine what it will be like!' This was an overwhelming thought, and it made me very happy. . . . This experience also had consequences for me. I had been bullied a lot in primary school. At that moment, I decided that the bullying had to end. And that happened."

This is a memory of an experience with immediate consequences, something which only occurs in older children. The boy or girl realizes his or her own uniqueness and independence and decides to live accordingly. Most experiences of younger children do not have such consequences, or these are not reported to me.

The realization of autonomy that accompanies this experience, of being in control over one's own body, one's own life, is something which I have encountered often in the memories people have sent me. Especially among older children.

Jung also talks about this impact of his individualization experience in the rest of the BBC interview. He suddenly felt 'an authority' ['*es war Autorität in mir*'] and started having doubts about the authority of his old-fashioned father over him.

The following memory concerns a slightly older girl. She is 15, and the reporting author is 49:

> "I would have been around fifteen and waiting for the tram (line 10, at the Rijksmuseum) to go home. In my memory, I was alone at this stop. I suddenly became aware of my body in a way I was not familiar with. I had a very clear sensation of living in this body, behind the skin, and that this was safe. My eyes were the windows

> through which I could observe the world. I never experienced this realization again."

One's own body as a safe home in which the *I* resides.

It is striking that there was no special trigger for this sudden self-awareness in these memories. The following memory of a middle-aged woman also lacks a trigger. The girl is not alone here, but with her family:

> "I remember realizing at a certain moment: 'I am alive'. I was around seven or eight, and it happened during dinner. I also remember the moment when my youngest brother had a similar experience, which also happened at the dinner table. He would have been around eight. He suddenly spread out his hands, looked at them, smiled enthusiastically and surprised, and said: 'Hey, I am alive!'"

This case is unique in my collection, as it reports a similar experience of both a brother and a sister.

The extraordinary aspect of this type of memory is that a child is struck by one's own body, which had always been there, but had never been noticed before. To give another example, a librarian remembers the following from back when she was 6:

> "I was sitting and playing a game on the floor in the hall in front of the bathroom. The house was completely quiet. I cannot remember whether I was home alone, but I had the feeling I was. Alone with myself. I looked at my hands and feet, my legs and toes, and suddenly realized that I was the one that made them move. I also used my voice in a variety of ways and knew that I was doing that myself. It was a feeling of great awe, but also of pride. Like I had power over myself. I could make myself do things. At the same time, I felt less connected with the people I knew."

Sudden awe and a feeling of pride about arms and legs that had always been there and had always been moved by the girl herself. But she only realized this when she was 6 years old.

The surprise about the fact that you are moving your own body reoccurs in the memory of a German woman:

> "I was around five years old and attending a nursery where all children had to sleep in the afternoon. I hated this, because there would

be a group leader sitting at a table to monitor us, and she was very strict. I was lying in the middle of the room on my bed. I was lying on my back and suddenly became aware of the fact that my stomach was moving up and down when I was breathing. This was the first time I became aware of my body and myself. It felt like I had an independent existence ['*irgendwie unabhängig existiere*']. But I also remember that this frightened me. I even rolled over onto my stomach. I had the feeling that this was something unpleasant that was only happening to me, not to the other children. I wanted to hide it. It was an anxious, but also fascinating experience which I remember in all its intensity."

In this memory, a child became aware of a certain aspect of her body: her stomach moving up and down. A body part is also enough to invoke the I experience in other memories in this 63-year-old woman also from Germany, for example. She was 5 years old at the time:

> "It was the summer of 1945, immediately after the war, and my parents held chickens in the basement because there was not enough food available in the stores, even though we lived in the city. Because this basement was quite high, it let in ample sunlight. There was a tray covered which chicken wire with newly born chicks. There was a hole in the wire at the top through which I could stick my hand. I was five and fascinated by the squeaking yellow chicks. I stuck my arm through the hole to catch and pet one. When she resisted, I pulled back my arm at once. A loose end of the wire poked into my arm and caused a wound which immediately started to bleed furiously. I stared at my arm and noticed that this was me for the first time. This was the first time I saw the pores of my skin, the white hairs, and the blood pouring out of me."

In this memory, the author looked at her own arm. However, the perspective can be even smaller: fingers and nails. Chicken wire also plays a role in this memory of an 86-year-old woman living in the United States:

> "It was 1941 and I was eight years and seven months. I can remember this precisely because it was two days before I caught scarlet fever and became terribly ill, which my parents would later tell me time and time again.
>
> I was standing on the sidewalk in front of a fence closing off a park with chicken wire in the middle. The wire had recently been tarred

and a few dried droplets were clinging to it. I do not remember how I ended up there, or who I was with. It felt like I was alone, but this could not have been the case for long. I broke off a droplet using my right thumb. I suddenly saw my thumb and nail and realized that this was my thumb and my nail. It was (and is) a beautiful nail, and I realized that I was very happy and satisfied, and independent from all the people I knew at that time. It was a quiet moment and lasted very briefly. But I looked differently at my friends and parents afterwards. I do not know exactly how I started looking at them, but it was different."

I want to conclude this chapter with two memories in which the female or male qualities of the body play a role. The first memory is from a woman aged 27 when she wrote me. She had only one younger sibling in her former household of six children and was the only girl. Her father told others that she was 'very much like a boy'.

> "When I was fourteen, I went to a reformed school, which was subject to strict rules. One of these rules concerned segregated physical education for boys and girls. This subject was quite unpopular, and many girls in my class would skip it by suggesting they were on their period. Since this trick worked very well, the number of permanently menstruating girls increased rapidly, resulting in a small number of girls actually attending the class, and a bench with around twenty girls having a fun time talking to each other. Our physical education teacher decided to give us a firm talking-to. He concluded his speech with the words: 'Do not abuse your womanhood.' These words had a great impact on me. All day, I kept thinking: 'I am a woman, I am actually a very young fourteen-year-old woman.' I was rejoicing about it all day: 'I am Marieke, and I am a woman!' I wrote it in my diary in the evening. Life seemed to have a different shade from that day on. Because I continuously realized: I am not a man, but a woman, I am a female human, I am a young woman. I kept thinking about it during the week after this experience, in class, in the train, everywhere. And I thought to myself: are all other girls experiencing the same thing? But I have never spoken about it to anyone."

Of course, Marieke already knew she was a girl and that girls ultimately become women. That must have been clear to her amidst all her brothers, even though she would sometimes act like a boy. She also knew that she had already started menstruating. But 'knowing' about these physical attributes had not yet led to an awareness of womanhood, of not being a man like her brothers, but of 'actually being a young woman'.

One of my assumptions about this type of 'awareness of being' is that they can occur in children whose parents did not often discuss intimate matters. If this girl would have been educated by her parents in the manner set out in all educational books, she likely would not only have realized that she was a woman based on a remark by her physical education teacher. To prove the authenticity of her memory, Marieke sent me a copy of the relevant page in her diary.

The second and last example is a bathroom memory of another young 34-year-old woman. The difference between masculinity and femininity is not expressed in the description, but remains implicit:

> "I would have been ten or eleven years old when I was in the bathroom together with my older brother. This was also one of the last times this actually happened. I believe it was even the very last time, since my brother was already going through puberty and preferred to lock the bathroom door. This is why I also remember how old I must have been during my I-am-I-experience. My brother was in the shower and I was sitting on the toilet when I suddenly had the strong realization that I am I, and he is he. It was so strong that I told it to my brother at that moment. He hardly responded to it, but I have been regularly reflecting on it my entire life, even now. I realized that my person and my body, but particularly my identity (which word I did not yet know at that time) in my body were entirely mine, and that nobody (my brother as the most obvious example at that moment) could replace these or could feel and experience what I was feeling and experiencing. At that same time, I realized that the same applied to my brother. That is also what I told him: 'You are you, and I am I, and you will never feel what I feel, and I will never feel what you feel.' Feeling in the broadest sense of the word: experiencing, living, thinking, and dreaming in your own way."

9

THE FIRMAMENT AND THE SUNLIGHT

It is remarkable that many individualization experiences of children are experienced in nature. In awe of the immense space of the firmament above them and their own place below it, sitting or standing the open field.

One of the first letters I received after my column in the Dutch newspaper *Trouw* offers a brief but precise description of the sensation of self-awareness in nature:

> "I could not have been older than nine, because we moved to a new house briefly after, and the environment would have been completely different. I was leaving school, the weather was great, and I went into a pasture to pick some flowers on my way home. The sky was bright blue, and the green color of the grass stood out to me, as well as the many flowers that were growing there. I was alone and did not see any other people anywhere around me. I stretched towards the sky, looking up, took a deep breath, and suddenly realized that I was 'someone'. Not merely one of the many children from my class, not simply one of the seven children of my parents, but an individual person. I remember a very happy and proud sensation, like I had discovered something very special.
>
> I did not tell this to anybody. It became like a 'secret' I could not express. I cannot remember any special events that could have triggered this discovery, but I do know that I reflect on this moment often and have this same extraordinary feeling every time.

I am now seventy-five. I now know – rationally – that each person is unique. But the discovery back then had nothing to do with any form of rationality."

The following memory of a 42-year-old woman is quite similar:

> "I also have had the experience of 'sudden insight'. Which is funny, because I thought I was the only one. I believe that I was seven or eight and in the second grade of primary school. We were living in Helmond at that time in a semi-detached home on an avenue. There was an undeveloped field next to our home which was mowed twice a year and unused otherwise, which will no doubt have been developed now. You could cross this field diagonally to and from school. And that is where it happened: an overwhelming feeling, during which I suddenly realized that I existed and that I was somebody else than others. It was a very awe-inspiring and beautiful feeling; I remember it very well. It was also a feeling of being chosen. I definitely started a new phase of my life from that day on. Later developments like a religious awareness, but also the simple ambition and need to make my life worthwhile, all originated from this day. I have never talked about this with anyone, maybe because it can easily sound pathetic."

The feeling of not only being independent, but also the sensation of being chosen, occurs more often in my collection. Because many of the authors of the letters and emails sent to me are somewhat older, the open-field experiences offer a nice description of what the Netherlands used to look like. A 60-year-old visual artist wrote:

> "As a boy I would attend a small village school. My fellow pupils were children of laborers, as was I. When I was twelve, I developed an extraordinary interest in nature, especially in birds. I would often wander through the fields. One afternoon, I was riding my bike to what is now called the 'Zaanse Schans'. Back in 1952, there were only a few black mills, without sails, there. I was riding on the narrow, winding path along the river Zaan, with a view of the wide polder on the right without any people around. I placed my bike in the grass and wandered around a bit. At that place, near the black mills, I experienced an overwhelming sensation. I saw myself standing in what I then experienced as an unmeasurable space, feeling like the firmament was expanding at the same time. It expanded in all

> directions, while I told myself: 'I am Gerbrand Volger.' I experienced this as a moment of awe."

'I saw myself standing there'. This memory could also have been in Chapter 7. That chapter discussed the phenomenon of a child looking at itself from a distance or a height.

But it is not only daylight that results in an overwhelming sensation of 'unity', standing underneath a starry sky often has the same effect. An artist said the following in an interview, pointing at a portrait of herself made by her father:

> "I was six years old. It was just before I became aware of myself. I still remember that moment very clearly. I was standing in the snow, alone, late at night. We lived on a road with large oaks and beeches. It was snowing and the lights were on, which made it look like everything was flickering. I was standing there alone, and I suddenly caught it, whatever it was. A feeling of uniqueness. Complete unity with myself. I still experience that same feeling sometimes when I step into a starry night."

A feeling of uniqueness, that is what I call the individualization experience, which is a phrase I have already used a number of times.

Being alone is not a mandatory condition for a natural experience, as it can also happen in the company of others, even though these experiences are rarer in my collection. Here is one:

> "I am eleven and in the sixth grade of primary school. I am sitting near the window. This is my first time I am in a classroom with very high windows. When I turn my head to the left a bit and look out of the window, I see light, space, openness. There are a number of thin trees on the grass immediately in front of the window. Behind it there is a road, followed by green pastures with some shrubs and trees. I can look very far, up to a castle, set against a dark forest. The river Vecht is also there, but I cannot see the water. But the most overwhelming of all of this is the sky above the land. Light blue with bright white clouds. I realize that this is very beautiful, and that the sky will always be there and will always look different. The sky will be there even when I am not looking. I realize that I am seeing the sky because **I** am looking at it. The sky exists because **I** am looking. The sky exists FOR ME, solely because I am looking at it. There is

no other way to look at it. At the same time, I am aware that the sky will still be there when I am not looking at it."

In another memory about an experience in nature, the child is not only outside in open space, but also at a height. A 45-year-old man wrote:

> "I was fourteen and in the small garden behind our home when I saw the sky in the west turn orange-purple on a warm autumn evening. Because I wanted to be able to see the full panorama, unhindered by clothesline poles and dove tills, I left my street and crossed the canal to a grass-covered sandy hill that lay there waiting for the construction of a new highway. I climbed it and looked at the colors of the setting red sun in awe. At the same time, the following thought filled me from head to toe: 'I am standing here, alone! Below me is the world, the village, our terrace home, the garden, my parents, my family, like in a world of mannequins. And I am standing here, alone with the sun, which will set soon, as I will climb down and be absorbed into the world of mannequins again.' The complete randomness of this moment fascinates me. Insofar as I can remember, there was no trigger for it."

Alone with the sun, outside in open space. The same thing happens in the memory of a 42-year-old woman:

> "I believe that I was merely five years old. This seems very young to me, but I believe that it is correct, because I was the bridesmaid at my aunt's wedding briefly thereafter. This wedding confirms the age I was at the time of this experience. . . . My parents and I had visited the aunt that was about to marry. When leaving her home, my parents continued to exchange a few words. I slipped through the talking trio and walked along the street a bit. The sun is shining into my eyes, the light blinding me, and I hold my arm in front of my head, just above my eyes. Once I walked along the street for a few meters, I turn around and see my parents and aunt talking and want to shout out to my parents to join me. Instead, I suddenly see and experience my parents as my parents, and myself as separated from them. I thought something like: 'I am one, and they are two. Two, one, two, one, two, one.' That is how my thoughts resonated, and how I stood paralyzed looking at those two people. (My aunt no longer plays any meaningful role in this memory from that moment).

> I experienced myself as alone, separated, as I am I. I remember that there was a very high tree somewhere to the right of the street that was illuminated by the sun. I can no longer remember the meaning of this tree, but it seemed like I was inspired by it at that time. The situation was interrupted when my parents shouted something and walked over to me. I was very happy while this was happening. I can still easily remember this sensation of happiness, but it never returned with the same intensity."

A German woman also remembers being happy when she discovered her 'self-awareness':

> "I was not quite six years old when I went outside on a summer morning. I leaned against the cool wall of our house, welcoming the warmth of the first rays of sun on my skin. I took a deep breath and thought about both the previous night and the warm day it was promising to become. I heard the birds sing and felt a lovely breeze. I was there on my own, and I was I, but one with everything at the same time. I felt the world around me, took a deep breath, and was happy and thankful for the moment. Later, I kept reflecting on this scene and believed for a long time that it was my first strong sensation of nature, but your article made me recognize the element of self-awareness in it."

The sun occurs often in these memories, including in the memories of the authors Vladimir Nabokov and Jacques Lusseyran in Chapter 3.

But the sun can also have an awe-inspiring presence indoors, such as in the following memory of a French author from back when she was 4 years old as recorded in her autobiography:

> "I was still a busy child full of excitement . . . when I was struck by a strange realization while running down the stairs one morning to play outside. The smell of the soft carpet on the stairs and a ray of sunlight enhanced by a yellow piece of stained glass made me freeze in place on a step, like I felt a hand on my shoulder. 'I am I', I whispered a short time later to my mother, who was surprised about the sudden change in my mood. . . . I clearly heard a voice say: 'Strange, that person who feels and looks, that am I!"[1]

Another example can be found in the memory of a 51-year-old Dutch woman:

> "We were on holiday in the countryside when I was almost seven years old. I remember the following fragment. I am sitting on the outside toilet, a small wood-clad room. There is a window behind me which lets in bright yellow sunlight at an angle. The sunlight illuminates the wooden wall to the right of me. The shelves are brown, coarsely sanded, with small protruding wood fibers. The sun also hits my lower arm. The small hairs, otherwise unnoticeable, have a golden hue in this light. I move my arm up and look at it. I think: 'This arm will no longer be here in eighty years.' I suddenly become aware of the fact that I am both this arm and not this arm at the same time. That I am my body, while I am also not my body."

I want to conclude this collection of experiences below the firmament or in the sun with a memory that did not take place in nature underneath the broad sky, but below the expanse of a large basilica. A child psychologist remembers the following from back when she would have been 7 years old, because she was wearing the blue dress of her first communion:

> "I had gone to the church by myself. It was quite early and there were only a few people in the large basilica-like church. I walked to the front through the central corridor from the back by myself. I was suddenly grasped by the overwhelming sensation of 'this-is-me' or 'I-am-walking-here', an intense feeling of self-awareness. This feeling has always stuck with me. It has to do with a very basic sense of self-confidence."

This psychologist also wrote that she was surprised by an article I wrote about this phenomenon:

> "I thought I was the only one for a long time. I had only encountered a description of such experience once before: in the novel *With open eyes* by Marguerite Yourcenar. The fact that I was also surprised by this book is clear from the fact I underlined the passage, a copy of which I have enclosed."

Note

1 Maria le Hardouin (1965) *Recherche d'une éternité*. Paris, Buchet.

10

PAST TIMES, FROM NOW TO THE END

Another type of sudden self-insight concerns the realization of time past, of becoming older, such as the realization that the world already existed before you and that it will end. Here is an example of a memory of a 48-year-old woman:

> "I was six years old. We were sitting at the table: my father, my mother, my two brothers, and me. My six-month-old sister was lying in her crib. We were eating and talking. I cannot remember what we were talking about. I suddenly realized that I had not always been there, that I had not always existed. I had not always been somebody with a father, a mother, and two brothers. That was shocking. I had simply always been there up to that moment. And this was suddenly no longer the case. I suddenly had to have had a beginning somewhere, had to have come from somewhere."

The awareness of passing time leads to an awareness of the 'self' in that time.

Triggers for a sudden expansion of the awareness of time are often one's own birthdays, which are very important milestones to a child who often eagerly looks forward to them, not only because of the expectation of gifts. A retired dentist, aged 75, remembers his sixth birthday in the Dutch Indies:

> "It was my sixth birthday when I was standing alone on the field in front of my home. I was looking at the traffic moving past, consisting

> mainly of walkers and cyclists. With this image in front of me, I suddenly had the following thought: 'The world is there, and I participate in it.'"

Another example is the birthday memory of a 64-year-old man:

> "I was walking in the Kazernestraat in Deventer on my tenth birthday, 17 May 1944. The street crosses the former Vesting canal. There was a square, iron railing at the side of the Handelskade. I let my hand slide over this railing, felt the warmth, and the small bubbles in the green paint. That is when I thought, or rather, that is when the following thought popped into my mind: 'I am Hans Lentink.' A bit farther along, where an asphalt road starts left to the water of the Handelskade, I thought: 'I could also have been a pig, but I am not, I am Hans Lentink.'"

This Hans would not have been a man if he did not immediately remark the following:

> "Now that I am reading this, I understand the hesitation with which I write this letter. It is just like a segment from a somewhat woolly book about which I am likely to think: 'Get over yourself.'"

However, he did overcome his apparent hesitations, as he added the following:

> "My parents may have put some emphasis on this tenth birthday. A pinnacle year in an exciting time, certainly to our family. I have always been aware of the fact that it was a decisive moment in my development, in my life. And I reflected on it numerous times in the period that followed. These thoughts were always accompanied by this amazement of not-merely-being-someone, and not being a pig – which made me very happy every time."

When I had to visit Deventer shortly after receiving this letter, I went to see whether this railing was still there. It was. The bubbles in the green paint were visible and could be felt. Only the iron was not warm, because it was January and raining. The asphalt path had been demolished briefly before, however. The entire area was being renovated, and this railing will by now have disappeared.

A Dutch actress also described her tenth birthday:

> "I am lying in my bed at night at nine years old. It is the day before my birthday. In previous years, I could not wait for the day to come. I was allowed to get into my mum and dad's bed and got lots of attention and presents. But this time I felt sad, I was tossing and turning. Something terrible was secretly going to happen tomorrow morning. I would be 10! I would suddenly belong to the double-digit club! The fact that I might reach triple digits at some point seemed like science fiction to me. Of course, I would be dead long before that. This made me feel even sadder. I wanted to stop the clock and hid under the blankets. Suddenly, some type of flashing light turned on in my mind, words flashing: I am I. A hesitant dialog started, someone started talking to me: 'Ineke, you can also take a different look at what is happening to you. In a different manner.'
>
> I sat up in the dark. 'Everything that will happen to you – a sudden thunderstorm, the cat walking away, crashing your bike, even your birthday – is simply fate. Or bad luck. You cannot do anything about it. You can only do something about your thoughts, the way you see things. You should not make yourself unhappy by thinking.' I got more and more excited, bright awake. It seemed quite logical to me: the external world will no longer decide for me, I can think for myself. Of course, I was not sure that would work out, but it did instill some confidence in me. I had a diary with a lock on which I had drawn two hands and written in a large font: 'Thieves stay away!!' I turned on a light, opened it, and wrote the following on 19 August 1953: 'Almost 10 years old. I hope that I will no longer feel unhappy. I will start thinking carefully from now on. Make my own decisions. Choose.'
>
> My parents congratulated me on my birthday the next morning. They were laughing: double digits, a milestone! I acted like it was a regular occurrence and unwrapped my gifts."

The sudden feeling of 'being your own boss' can also be found in the memory of a young woman:

> "I had just turned seven and am lying in bed in the morning underneath an orange bed sheet with white daisies. There is an orange bed light with three glass stars inside it above me. I suddenly realize that I am seven, which feels like the most important fact in the entire

world. I feel the fabric of my duvet cover, am aware of the space the length of my body occupies, and that it is my hand that can reach the light switch. I suddenly realize that I can change things in this room, such as folding my duvet back. It feels very significant, very free, to be seven, to be me, and not someone else."

Besides birthdays, celebrations of the end of the year with the change of date can be a reason to think about the progress of time in one's own life and the accompanying self-awareness. An example of this can be found in the memory of a German social work student:

> "I was around ten years old when I looked out of the window in the kid's room on New Year's Eve. I thought about what would happen in the new year, which would start in a few hours. Thinking about the future in this way, I suddenly wondered what would happen tomorrow. When I noticed that I had no idea what I meant with the word 'tomorrow', even though I used the word with the greatest ease, just like the people around me. But at the same moment, I suddenly did understand the meaning of 'tomorrow', 'yesterday', and 'today'. I had the feeling that I had been living in a dream when it came to these words. I suddenly understood their meaning beyond a rational level, just like you can suddenly understand the system behind mathematical fractions, even though these took so much effort up to that moment. No, it rather felt like I was amidst these words. That I would 'enter' the tomorrow from yesterday through today, and that this gave me continuity, even though I did not know that word at the time."

Continuity as self-awareness in time. Something similar can also be found in the memory of a 40-year-old woman from back when she was 8:

> "I underwent my first communion in 1967. It was common practice to give all guests that would come up to congratulate me a keepsake. A picture was taken of me, and I wrote the date '23 May 1967' on the back many times over.
>
> I was helping my parents at their company on a day late in December that same year. I was carrying a box to the place where I had to stack them. I can remember precisely where I was standing. We were busy due to the end of the year, and I knew that the new year would be 1968. I realized that if I were to do communion in that

> year and would have to write cards, I would be writing '1968'. This resulted in the sudden realization that time passes, that 1967 would never return after the end of the year, that time progresses in one direction. From that moment, I would look at time differently. It did not seem to have existed before that moment, even though I had my birthday every year and had become older each year. The calendar only started for me on that day in December 1967."

The girl in the following memory of the end of the year is also 8 years old. But she does not only have the awareness of, but also the associated sadness about the passing of things, and a first attempt to fight against this:

> "It was the last day of the year of 1975. It was suddenly like I was alone in the room for a moment. I saw myself standing, as it were, and thought: 'This moment will never return.' It will be 1976 tomorrow, and today will be over. I will no longer remember this after many years have passed. Both who I am now and what I am feeling. I had some difficulties with this, a sense of sadness. And I suddenly had the strong urge to hold on to it. That feeling, that moment. I did this by repeating the following words to myself: 'It is now the last day of the year of 1947, and I am eight years old. I am standing here, and so are the chairs and the table. Everything is like it is.' I stopped thinking for a moment to hold on to this. I cannot remember what I did afterwards. The strange thing is that this thought made me happy for a moment, and that I would go on with a sense of self-awareness, at least during that evening. It was like I figured something out that was essential to me."

She added the following about this memory:

> "This memory came back to me when I read your article. I have had little memories of my childhood for the longest time, until I had children myself. But then also returned the bad memories, and that could be confusing. And this is such a valuable memory of me as a child that I wonder how it ever ended up hidden so far away."

Some readers will have difficulties seeing such a seemingly unimportant event as something valuable. But I feel like it is extraordinary that a child discovers how you can fight the human sadness about the passing of time by capturing the fleeting episode in your mind. The child feels happy and strong for a moment because it believes it can do something about the fleeting nature of time. Could it not be possible that our urge to take pictures and record video stems from the same need? Is it not an attempt to hold on to what will soon disappear over the horizon of time? And what about keeping diaries, an archive, recording history? A young woman from Antwerp also tried to capture time:

> "When I was around nine to ten years old, I was standing in the basement underneath my parents' home. I remember that I was not doing anything special, until the moment I was standing in front of a table against the wall. There was a white, rectangular butter dish on the table with the paper film removed. I threw something lying next to the dish in it, a shell, rock, or marble, I cannot remember precisely. While I did this, I promised myself to remember this 'stop' in my life forever. I was clearly aware of the fact that I was living NOW, where I was standing, and also of the fact that I was a child and would not remain so forever. It was also a test to see whether you could always remember such a minor event, even in my old age. It did stay with me forever, and I am still happy that I can hold on to this memory now that I am thirty-two."

She added the following reflection:

> "I believe that this is the only way for me to truly prove that I existed as a child, to have had a grasp on the fleeting nature of life. It is like pinching your cheek to feel everything is actually real."

A German agricultural engineering student also tried to capture time as a 10-year-old:

> "My parents, brother, and I made the journey in our Trabant and drove through some beautiful landscapes. We stopped somewhere along the way and sat underneath a large, old tree. My brother and I were constantly walking around the tree and playing games. All of a sudden, I stood still, and carefully looked at everything surrounding me. I watched what the others were doing, how they were laughing, how the leaves moved in the wind, and how the rays of sun were shining through the branches. Then I was startled back to reality. I suddenly realized that I would never experience this beautiful moment again. I thought to myself how quickly time was passing and how quickly time had already passed. On that day, I made

> a promise to myself that I would think back to that moment every few years. I first reflected on that moment after hardly an hour had passed and we were continuing our journey in the Trabant. . . . This experience is so deeply engraved in my mind that I can still conjure up the image of the tree. I can see the narrow road and the field on the other side where the corn grows. I can see the house behind the tree and the bench right next to the tree."

In some memories, the awareness of time is even linked more closely to one's own self-awareness, the awareness of being. It can be found in this memory of a 52-year-old psychologist, for example:

> "It happened when I was around twelve to thirteen years old. I was reading a book for girls – I can no longer remember which one – and while reading the right page, at around a third of the way down, between two paragraphs, I suddenly had the overwhelming and shocking awareness of myself in the present, against the background of time itself, both the past and the future. The following sentence popped into my mind: 'Now is now, and she found this hard to grasp.' I spent some time – maybe a minute or two – exploring this thought in awe before I continued reading. I saw and felt myself more rooted in the present like this was something very special, but I could not understand it."

This psychologist also tried to analyze the meaning of this episode in her letter:

> "I now wonder whether it had more to do with a sense of self-awareness than the awareness of time. The funny thing is, I have always had the feeling of 'and she found this hard to grasp'. It clearly indicated that I was also looking at myself as an outsider, like I was reading a book about a schoolgirl going through such an experience. I later realized that it most likely was because of the various worlds in which I lived. They were all just as a real at the moment I was experiencing them, but they would sometimes intersect: the world of my books, my fantasy world, and the 'real' world. At the moment of my flash of awareness, I was apparently in both the real world and in the world of my books. . . . I still very rarely experience this same sensation as back then, but with less intensity, a sudden awareness of myself in the present against the background of time itself, like I

> disconnect myself from the past and the present. This always involves the same phrase: 'Now is now, and she found this hard to grasp.' The sensation always lasts briefly, and I still do not understand it."

These words are by a psychologist who never told anyone about this extraordinary experience for a period of 40 years, even though she often reflected on it during her life, as she informed me. This includes during and after her psychology studies to her colleagues, or to her husband or children. However, she was fine with me sharing her experience here.

Is it not remarkable that she never encountered similar experiences of children during and after her studies in the many books and articles she was required to read? I just can't understand that.

The *observing I* steps away from the occupied *being I* that lives in the here and now. This *observing I* in turn tries to distance itself from the passing time in which the *being I* lives. It is able to do so for a moment up to a certain degree, but this *observing I* is also bound to the passing of time.

It strongly reminds me of an image I used to conclude my oration many years ago, derived in part from the Russian author Nadezhda Mandelstam:[1]

> "We are dragged along by streams. We sometimes have the chance to grab a branch hanging over the river to hold on to for a moment and pull ourselves up from the water. For a moment, we want to know where we are, where we came from, where we are going. It is possible to see some things, but not too much. And then, 'Splash!', we continue onwards."

This passage is about the flow of time from which the *observing I* emerges, becomes aware of this flow for the first time, as if it were taking a picture or recording a video to try and capture the present. But this moment of the present changes immediately. The present cannot be captured. Now-now is no longer then-now. Now-now does not really exist, and the famous phrase 'now is now' is not true in that sense, as it is not compatible with the actually flowing and ever-changing present. Is this why our psychologist is still unable to understand her own short phrase, conjured up by a 12-year-old girl?

'Now is now' seems like an obvious truth, but it is impossible to understand if you actually explore the thought. It has passed the moment you try to grasp it. It can be represented or described on a picture or in a film, a diary, or a poem, but the image or description is not the same as this 'now'.

You sometimes hear people say: 'Now is now, and then was then' to indicate that they do not value experiences from the past. Yes, then was then, that is hard to argue with. But now is no longer now, and that can be difficult to understand. This is described beautifully by a 6-year-old girl:

> "I was standing in the bathroom in front of the sink. The curtain of the window next to me was closed. It let in some diffuse green light. The mirror above me reflected the world, as did the white ceramic of the sink, albeit not as clearly. Outside, a car drove past, and I heard the sound of cups in the kitchen. I suddenly heard and saw all of this very intensely and thought something like: 'I am standing here now, at this moment, but everything will be gone in a bit. I can stand here again later, but it will not be the same.'"

I also received a few memories from people – one man, all the rest women, I cannot help it – who as a child realized that their childhood would not last forever, or that their childhood was over. I want to give a memory of my wife as an example:

> "I had just started to attend High School. An opening gala was organized in the auditorium at the start of the academic year. All students who wanted could perform there. I had gained some renown in reciting poems at primary school. My older sister attended presentation lessons. Reflecting on this, I think this is what inspired me. I cannot remember with which poem I signed up for the gala. But I remember the following very clearly, even though I have never spoken about it with anyone. I enter the auditorium that afternoon during the final rehearsal. Through the central corridor with the organ at the end. Boys from higher grades are practicing with their band below the organ. A tall blond boy is playing the drums. It is difficult to capture my feelings in words. But I suddenly realized with absolute certainty: 'I cannot recite a poem here. That is childish. And I am no longer a child. I now belong to this type of guys.' The idea that they would hear me reciting that poem filled me with shame. I walked directly to the teacher directing the show and told him I had a terrible throat ache. He thought that I was suffering from stage fright and laughed at me a bit. I did not care, avoiding a fate that would be many times worse."

And then the passing of time comes to an end. A young woman realizes this in a prosaic manner at the age of 5:

> "My mother had a recipe book. There was a chocolate pudding on the cover. A beautiful one, a shiny shell made of dark-brown chocolate, which you can never remove from the mold so perfectly yourself. I was around five years old, a great fan of puddings, and this one intrigued me greatly.
>
> We had a new fixed rotary clothesline in our yard. I would play my favorite game there whenever my mother used it to dry our white sheets. Looking at the shadows of the sheets on the grass. And waiting for the sun to disappear and pop up again to create new shadows.
>
> Two seemingly random facts from an ordinary childhood, but they were given significance in a dream which I can remember vividly even now. I was playing outside in the sun, and my mother was hanging the sheets on the rotary clothesline. Shadows came and went, but they would suddenly stay away. The sun had changed into a chocolate pudding, a shiny, dark-brown shell. It became dark out and stayed that way, even when I woke up crying. I was alone in bed and suddenly realized: 'Even the sun can disappear. One day, it will fail to rise.' The realization of the finiteness of existence had crashed into my life with an enormous impact."

Self-awareness will sometimes arise in a child when it is confronted with the irrevocable end, with death. Becoming aware of your mortality is accompanied by the awareness of one's own self. A Dutch sculptor wrote the following about this:

> "It was a beautiful day and the window of our living room was wide open. My father was sitting in his chair next to the window. I was standing next to him. I must have been around four years old. My mother was wandering around the room. I cannot remember why, but they were talking about dying: 'Everyone will die eventually'. When asked if I would too, they answered yes. This announcement hit me quite hard. Surely, that could not be true. It did not apply to me. I would continue on living. I looked at the blue sky outside, as if the immeasurable space outside needed to confirm that my life was eternal. But I still believed my parents. After all, they knew

> everything. This belief left me with a feeling of sadness. They tried to say encouraging things to me, but it did not help. One day I would die."

The autobiographical childhood memories of a female theologian and author of children's books also contain an early and sudden realization of the inevitability of the later death of herself. She calls herself Hetty and writes about herself in the third person in these memories. Her biographer calls it her 'first self-experience'. She was staying with an aunt, who told her that her grandfather had passed away. Hetty was 10 years old at the time:

> "That was impossible, she believed. Nobody had told her anything about her grandfather being ill. You cannot die suddenly. So abruptly. Hetty did not cry. She looked at her aunt in an almost hostile manner. Her aunt did not become angry. She told Hetty that her grandfather had been very old and weak, and that his death was not entirely unexpected. And that she did not need to be sad. She gave Hetty a kiss, turned off the light, and left. Hetty was lying in the dark. Death, death, death, death, death, she said, until it made her cry. She kept crying for a while and thought 'Later, when I am old and have experienced much sadness, I will die'."[2]

Notes

1 Nadezhda Mandelstam (1971) *Hope Against Hope*. New York, Random House.
2 Johanna Kuiper (1934) *Kinderherinneringen*. Utrecht, Bijleveld.

11
MIRRORS

Almost all parents let their young children look at themselves in the mirror asking them what they were seeing. Or they are too impatient to wait for the answer and tell them: 'Look, that is . . .', calling out the name of the child. The same happens with pictures and videos on smartphones nowadays. At some point, the young child will call out its name when seeing itself like this. The parents are happy and believe that their child is showing self-awareness. But what does this awareness actually constitute?

The development of thinking about oneself is a complicated affair. As an example, I cite the observations the Swiss psychologist Jean Piaget made of his little daughter Jacqueline.[1]

He had come to believe that the girl, who was barely 2 years old at the time, could recognize herself in the mirror. And so he was surprised when one time after taking a walk with her father and her sister, Jaqueline said that she 'wanted to see daddy, Odette and Jacqueline in the mirror', as if the Jacqueline in the mirror had an existence apart from her own.

One year later, the girl saw a picture of herself asleep on Piaget's back and leaning against his shoulder during a mountain walk. Pointing to herself, she asked anxiously, 'Oh, what's that? I am afraid of it'. Piaget answered, 'But who is it? Can't you see?'

'Yes', she said, 'it's me. Jacqueline is doing this [imitating the sleeping attitude]. So she is not afraid'.

The next day, Piaget showed her another picture of herself and asked her who it was. 'It's Jacqueline'.

Her father asked her, 'Is it you or not?'

'Yes, it's me, but what has that Jacqueline got on her head?'

So it was her, but it also wasn't her. At this early age, there is no clear and stable understanding of one's own identity vis-à-vis changing images on pictures taken in different circumstances, in different clothes, and at different ages.

But nevertheless, some young children looking into a mirror are capable of self-recognition, as can be illustrated with an observation cited by the child psychologist Michael Lewis.

> 'David is a two-year-old who loves helping his mother bake brownies. Being a little overenthusiastic, he gets more flour on his hands than in the bowl and is asked to go and wash up. Upon looking in the mirror over the sink, he discovers to his glee that there is flour on his cheek, and he tried to wipe it off with his hand.'[2]

Observations like this inspired Lewis and his colleagues to an extensive series of laboratory experiments using the technique developed by Gordon Gallup in his work with chimpanzees and other nonhuman primates. Gallup surreptitiously placed some dye on the animal's nose and observed its behavior in front of the mirror. Did the animal make a movement toward the face in the mirror as if seeing another animal or toward his own nose, as if noticing 'there is something with *me*'?

Of all primates tested, only chimpanzees were clearly able to recognize and direct their actions to the marks on their own faces.

Using the same technique Lewis and his colleagues found that infants from 15 to 24 months of age touched their faces when placed in front of a mirror after their faces were surreptitiously marked with rouge.

Between 18 and 24 months, a significant increase occurred, with approximately 75 percent of the 18-month-olds and all of the 24-month-olds exhibiting the recognition of the mark as something on their own face.

Lewis sees these earliest forms of self-recognition as the dawning of the 'objective' self- awareness, in which the child's mind perceives the self as an 'object'. It is the next step after the stage in which the child's mind reacts to signals from the position senses, such as protecting himself or herself from falling down the stairs.

The absolute certainty is established at a later age: this face in the mirror is my face. But then a new uncertainty may arise, this time about the characteristics hidden in or behind the image shown in the mirror: Do others see me and value me as I do? My collection does not include memories of adults who came to a sudden self-awareness when looking into the mirror as a child. I only know of one example in literature, by the French author Marguerite Yourcenar:

> "I remember looking at myself in the mirror back when I was around eight – as I attempt to reconstruct the situation based on the clothes and furniture around me – and telling myself: 'Look, I am, I am important, those others have no clue about this.' 'Those others', that was everyone, in all my surroundings. A strange certainty – as I was rather quite humble by nature as a child . . . and I believe that something of this predisposition still remains to this date – , a strange certainty of being someone. A vague idea of fame, too."[3]

Besides the fact that this is an example of a child whose self-awareness arises while looking into a mirror, there is also the hint of the discovery of a certain autonomy, 'I am important', even a vague idea of future fame. But the statement that 'others have no clue about this' is interesting as well. This is an aspect described in the mirror-related memories of some of the subjects in my collection. They had already come to self-awareness at this point. The mirror in this situation is the trigger for a literal reflection on this self: I am more and different than how others see me. Others see my appearance, just like I see it in the mirror right now. But there is more, but I am the only one who knows this as it is hidden to others. An older psychologist wrote, for example:

> "When I was nine, I started considering myself a grown-up boy; I belonged to the tallest of my school year. I had hardly any ideas about who or what I was. But I started observing myself from around that time. When my parents were away from home, I would sit at the edge of their bed to look at myself in the large vanity mirror of my mother. Not very often, but sometimes. One time, I thought: 'I can now see myself how others see me, and how I see others . . . but there is something missing, something which cannot be seen. There is a lot more in me, an entire world that cannot be seen from the outside.' This world filled with thoughts and feelings was very real to me, and I may very well have been more of that world than my external appearance. And that is how I came to the following discovery: 'I am inside that body, and actually invisible.' This discovery made a deep impression on me."

A Dutch poet and illustrator describes something similar in one of his novellas but takes another step: the mirrors are false! He told me that he gave this personal memory to his 13-year-old main character:

> "I always feel like mirrors are wrong when I look in them. Because I know that I actually look different. More ordinary. With smaller ears. Older. My real face does not reveal my thoughts as clearly. Nobody would laugh at me if I would look like myself, for example. Mirrors are fools. I should have a calm, ordinary face that never changes. Mannequins in the stockings store have such faces. . . . I thought that mirrors would become more accurate as you age. I am almost thirteen now, and there is still no mirror that is correct."[4]

It is actually not that surprising that the internal I-am-I experience is so rare when looking into a mirror. When looking at one's own body, one's own face, you can only see the external self. It is a literal look at yourself, always more or less randomly and casually observed, sometimes studied with a greater level of attention due to a striking new detail – a wound, bags below your eyes, running mascara.

But mirrors can be a trigger for a first moment when a child who already has self-awareness, who already feels like a person, starts thinking about himself or herself. The ideas that are triggered by this reflection can make such an impression that they are given a lasting place in one's mind. In the two examples set out earlier, the thoughts lead to greater insight: I am more and different than what you can see in the mirror, more and different than what others can see in me. The visible appearance is lacking validity compared to the knowledge you have about yourself, is less rich and less true.

In a personal memory from back when I was 10 or 11 years old and lived in the Hague, I can see myself in front of a washbasin with a mirror above it. I am naked and washing myself. I am alone in the room. The curtains are drawn and the door to the landing is closed (but not locked). I had recently been given this private room at the front of the house. Until then, I had shared a room with a few of my brothers. Our household counted six children.

I become aware – with some degree of awe – of the simple fact that I am washing myself in the isolation of this private room. The memory is *innocent of words*, and when I look for the words to express the substance of my self-awareness of this moment to another person, I sense that I am wrong. The moment is without any emotions, there is no fear, no sense of loneliness. My parents, brothers, and sisters do not play a role, at least not in the foreground of this memory; maybe in the background as a trigger. There is no conscious relationship with eroticism or sexuality, no discovery of my own body as a source of lust. The strongest sensation is the association with the awareness of privacy and autonomy, of being in control, undoubtedly related to the isolation in this own private room for the first time in my life.

The question arises: Does this mirror not play a role? No, not really, I am not looking at my own reflection. In my memories, I can still see a bit of the front of my body, as Hughes wrote about his Emily.

But why did I remember this event of more than 70 years ago? So many things have disappeared from my long-term memory, many more things than I can remember. So why did I remember this? The sense of awareness at this unique moment must have made such an impression, and this impression must have been embedded in my memory to such an extent that it never faded away with all the other memories that have disappeared. The experience must have had some 'impact', but there is no emotional sensation. I can very clearly remember certain emotional events, accompanied with great fear, sadness, and anger from this period. If standing in front of the mirror and the washbasin did invoke emotions, I would have remembered them.

The experience was not only wordless, but it was also emotionless. It likely was merely an intense awareness of being an individual person.

Notes

1 Jean Piaget (1945/1962) *Play, Dreams and Imitations in Childhood.* New York, Norton & Company.
2 Michael Lewis (1992) *Shame: The Exposed Self.* New York, The Free Press.
3 Marguerite Yourcenar (1984) *With Open Eyes: Conversations with Matthieu Galey.* Boston, Beacon Press.
4 Harrie Geelen (2004) *Het nijlpaard ellende.* Amsterdam, van Oorschot.

12

EXTRAORDINARY EXPERIENCES OF JOY

During a sudden I-am-I experience, a child looks at itself in surprise. But I have also received memories in which a child or young person felt the *I* gets absorbed into something 'higher', something which actually far transcends the self. It was still a sudden event, but not exactly like the experiences I was looking for. It is not that I consider those experiences less important than those I have described in the previous chapters. But I cannot categorize them as insights with general applicability. As a psychologist, those patterns in childhood development are what I am looking for. Everyone develops self-awareness, and I am looking at how this suddenly breaks through in some children. Transcendent experiences are in fact too personal to be able to be categorized. Many people do not experience them, and there is great variety among the people who do. Everyone experiences 'the transcendent sensation' differently. I do want to give a few examples, however, because they are beautiful.

I will start with a memory by the well-known Dutch author Godfried Bomans from when he was an adolescent:

> "I remember being in the yard one evening after dinner and sitting underneath the hawthorn with my back against the stem and my knees pulled towards my chest: it was between light and dark, all noises were dying off, and the silver moon calmly rose between the naked branches. And it was suddenly like time, the moment, fell from my shoulders (I cannot properly express what happened exactly), and

> I was lifted up into an entirely different manner of being; it was like I became thinner but also endlessly larger and wider, so wide that I filled the entire night around me, and that the night itself and the things in it became one and I understood 'everything'."[1]

Lifted up into an entirely different manner of being. Something comparable, 'feeling enveloped' can be found in the memory sent to me from England by a Dutch female therapist:

> "I must have been between seven and nine years old when I was walking home one day near my primary school. I was alone and can almost remember the exact location where I had this experience. I was standing on the blue curb, ready to cross the road, when I was struck by something. It was like I was lifted upwards. This experience, which felt like something was 'enveloping' me, was charged with a force and energy I could not define. I felt lifted upwards and enveloped by an energy and – how to describe it – . . . love, even though I did not realize this at the time. I felt a force of belonging to something, like I was part of a larger whole of which I was at the center. When the moment passed, I felt like I had been completely out of this world for a moment."

Feeling 'enveloped', love, energy. These are the words used to describe this transcendent experience. The following memory revolves around beauty. A remedial child psychologist responded to my call with the following 'break-through experience', as she calls it:

> "I was eight years old and I was in the woods of Wassenaar together with my brother. I walked away from him and ended up in an area of the forest I did not know. I suddenly saw a large bush of rhododendrons in full bloom, as if I ended up in a fairytale. The beauty of the flowers, hit by the sunlight, gave me an overwhelming experience. I realized, very strongly and without any doubts: this is beauty, and I am the only one who sees it. There was a sensation of complete unity between me and nature. This experience has stuck with me my entire life, and still fills me with a tremendous sense of joy whenever I think about it."

A tremendous experience, like in a fairytale, leading to complete unity. 'Complete harmony with my surroundings' is how art critic Henk van Os calls it in a letter sent to me. Just like Godfried Bomans, he was sitting with his arms around his knees. He was leaning against a church tower, while Bomans was leaning against a tree:

> "In the fifties, my parents would take their children to Lenz in the Engadin (Switzerland) each holiday. We would stay with the headteacher of the village who taught us mounting climbing and Schweizer-German. One evening, I had been given permission to go for a walk alone after dinner. Outside of the village, there was an isolated Roman St Mary's Church on a hill between the high mountains. The church contained a beautiful central altarpiece with radiant golden statues. They were made of wood and gilded, but that did not matter. The church was surrounded by gravestones that often listed the names of the headteacher and his wife: Semeon-Willi or Willi-Simeon. I sat down against the church tower and looked at the mountains. I firmly hugged my knees into my chest. Gradually, I was overcome by a sensation of joy. I was sitting here, away from all others. This was my domain. My arms held my knees tightly. I later learned a German phrase for this: Sich zusammen nehmen. But the actual extraordinary sensation was that I felt in complete harmony with my surroundings at the same time as this I-am-I-experience. I wanted to stay like this forever. This had to do with the view over the mountains, but probably also with my isolated position, virtually tucked against the house of God. God certainly played a role. I was a very religious young boy back then, very much in the spirit of 'God is very great, and I am very small.'"

The I-am-I experience is mentioned briefly but somewhat casually. The focus is on what he wrote me somewhat later:

> "Overwhelming everything was a feeling of gratitude, limitless gratitude, which was released by this experience."

The experiences previously mentioned could be called 'cosmic', assimilating into an undefinable 'AI'. But such joyful assimilation into a larger whole can also be more grounded. A woman, aged 82, wrote the following about herself from back when she was 3 years old:

> "I wake up, and am aware that I am lying in the box-bed while the yellow flickering oil light occasionally casts shadows and muffled voices come from the other room, accompanied with the sound of crackling. My brother, who is almost a year older, had been gifted a swing which my father had installed in the pantry. The crackling

> noise came from the thick rope. I was overcome by a sensation of joy and assurance. I am lying here, I am part of it, part of the light, the noise, everything. I have never expressed it before, but this type of yellowish light would always fill me with a sensation of joy afterwards, such as the light of the old street lanterns in Paris."

Such enviable experience of assurance, of being part of a greater structure, the family, is substantively different from the experiences of self-awareness and individuation that the previous chapters focus on. Just like in the memory previously mentioned, the following memory of a woman also revolves around the larger structure of the family in which the child finds love and assurance:

> "I was nine and had just stopped believing in Santa Claus. This was the first time I could join the evening festivities. Because I still had a sister who believed in Santa Claus, I had agreed with my parents that I would wait until she was asleep, as we used to sleep in the same room. Afterwards, I would tiptoe down the stairs. I still have a vivid memory of standing at the top of the stairs while the rest of the world was waiting for me. I was filled with a great sense of expectation, which I also realized. I thought: 'This is happiness. I am going downstairs to people who love me and we will do something great.' I could hear the bustle and smelled hot chocolate. At that moment, I also thought: 'I need to cherish this moment, it is too large for now, I need to store it away somewhere.' That is why I stood there for at least a minute. I looked at the white wall in front of me, focusing on a small red smear. I closed my eyes to absorb the touch of the railing. I very deliberate focused on the smell of hot chocolate. Then I went downstairs."

The experiences set out in this chapter and the experiences described in the previous chapters share the intense feeling of self-awareness, which can also be called 'sensations of self-awareness'. However, they contain substantive differences, as they are not focused on the *I* as a unique individual and the difference between this *I* and others, but actually on the relationship with the other, nature, 'the greater and broader whole'.

Note

1 Godfried Bomans (1993) *Dagboek van een gymnasiast: Vroege jeugdherinneringen*. Amsterdam, De Boekerij.

13

OTHER SUDDEN INSIGHTS

A young child lives in a world full of uncertainties in many ways. When it grows up, it must step away from many of these and face reality. Things that were self-evident actually turn out to be different. They also make surprising discoveries.

I received two about the discovery that the world turned out to be larger than the child realized until that time. I assume that such memories can no longer arise suddenly nowadays, because children drive all across the country on the backseats of cars and fly to other states and countries during holidays. Almost no toddlers grow up with only the familiarity of their own immediate surroundings. These memories offer a glance at how young children used to grow up in the Netherlands after World War II:

> "On the Sunday on which I discovered the world, I went to visit two sisters of my father, aunt Trees and aunt Agatha, together with my father, mother, and brothers, just as we used to do every Sunday during that time, the early thirties. They lived in Bolsward, just like us, and traded in women's lingerie and all related products. My parents drunk coffee and we were given a glass of lemonade with some gingerbread from the bakery. Aunt Agatha was reading to us and aunt Trees was talking with my parents. A recurring topic was the comic in the number of the last week of the regional magazine.

That Sunday, the aunts told us that they were planning on cycling to Scharnegoutum that afternoon. I asked what Scharne-goutum was. Scharnegoutum, said aunt Trees, is a village behind Sneek. The world opened up to me at that moment. There was more than just Bolsward and Sneek and the pastures between them. You could go farther. And the world surely did not end at Scharnegoutum, you could keep going. It was a dazzling discovery."

A similar discovery was somewhat frightening in the next memory:

"I was around eight years old. We had visited my grandfather and grandmother. My father, mother, sister, and I were in the car on the way home. It was evening and it was dark out. I was drifting in and out of sleep and looked out of the window occasionally. I can remember the moment and my feelings vividly, like I am looking at myself in that car from up above. I looked outside and saw many lights in the distance. First, I thought that these were all created by lantern poles, but there were so many above each other. I asked my parents why there were so many lights there. They told me they were created by houses that were built upon each other and that people lived there. This shocked me greatly. How was that possible? Until that time, my world consisted of separate one-store village houses and I hadn't yet seen apartment-buildings. But there was more! I experienced this as a threat, but also felt curious."

The following two memories concern the belief in God:

"It was the morning of my tenth birthday, and I would be able to point out the exact location in the classroom where I was sitting when I suddenly realized that there were people others considered so evil they simply had to die. I had heard that Adolf Eichmann had been given the death penalty in Jerusalem and would be hanged. I felt that this would not be discussed with me at home, because they considered me way too young for this, as was the case for many topics. What the man had done, which evil he represented, I did not know, only 'that it had to do something with the war'. I was raised with the idea that you could only die if God wanted it. But apparently, people could also decide this! The idea bounced around in my mind my entire birthday, but I believe that the day was quite fun otherwise."

A great example of the sudden disappearance of certainty. Another Dutch woman suddenly became aware of the difference between a loving God and a loveless church when she was around 12 years old:

> "I was born halfway through the fifties and was raised in a provincial city, which had various strongly segregated Christian denominations. I grew up in a rather strictly believing family. Even though my parents were very guarded when criticizing other protestants, there was a general mood of: we belong to 'the chosen people', and those other churches have to prove themselves. From the age of around ten, I was very worried about all those people that would be 'lost' because of their misfortune of attending the wrong church. This idea did not agree with what we were told about a loving God. One day, I was walking in the middle of the city and ended up on one of the bridges across the river IJssel. From there, I could look into four directions and counted no less than seven churches with church towers. Suddenly I was struck by the thought that God could not consider only one of these to be the correct one. This thought frightened me, because it was some form of heresy. At the same time, I felt an enormous internal liberation."

Children usually learn to always speak the truth. And they rely on the certainty that parents do so. In the next memory, a child suddenly discovers the relativity of this:

> "I must have been around seven years old. I was the youngest in my family and one of my two older brothers had done something he should not have. I no longer remember what exactly. When my mother asked who had done it, none of us gave an affirming answer. All three of us were sent upstairs to put pressure on the 'perpetrator'. Once the perpetrator would come forward, the others could come downstairs as well. I called out to my mom: 'If I had done it, I would have said so!' I first felt a bit sad in my room. My mother did not believe me and I was unfairly sent upstairs. While I was stubbornly thinking about this, I realized that if I had actually done something, I could simply say I had not: I could lie! I felt triumphant about this discovery the rest of the day."

Other events that can be of enormous importance to children concern the sudden insight into what they can do well and what not, insight into their own talents. The following memory concerns something that perfectively illustrates the fact that so many children aged around 7 to 8 can create fantastic and creative drawings and paintings, but that they stop doing so quite suddenly and start considering the works praised and displayed by their parents and grandparents to be childish. They lose the naive attitude toward their own work, start to see the difference in quality between what they create and how things and people 'really' look like, or between their work and drawings in a book. Reality intrudes at the expense of their fantasy. The following child compares her drawing to what she imagined to be a colorful and lively representation of 'reality'. This makes this memory unique and important. How could one ever identify such a thought at such a young age using the regular methods of scientific developmental psychology?

> "I was seven years old and sitting in the middle of the classroom, which had three rows of benches. My teacher, Mr. Altink, had enthusiastically told a story off the top of his head and we had been instructed to draw the aspect of the story that made the strongest impression on us. I immediately saw what I was going to draw in front of me. A clear image. I would draw the little white lambs in a green pasture with clover and a dark wolf approaching the herd from behind. It was a clear day in spring and the sun would radiate from my drawing. I opened my large box of Carandache crayons and started in the tense expectation that I would create something very beautiful. But while drawing my first lamb, I painfully realized that the animal did not at all look like how I imagined it, and I suddenly knew that I would not succeed in this for the time being. It was the first time I looked at my drawings with an 'objective' look and saw my incapability. I felt very disappointed."

The loss of certainties and an upcoming realistic approach toward one's own capabilities are in contrast with the discoveries of the powerful instrument of language. I received memories about the moment on which the meaning of a word suddenly became clear, even though the child had heard and used it often before. A Dutch psychiatrist described the moment at which, well at the age of 4, he gained insight into the difference between *eindeloos* (endlessly) and *eindelijk* (finally):

> "In a Japanese internment camp during World War II, in the former Dutch Indies, I was housed in a bamboo warehouse with a roof

> made of palm leaves together with my mother. Women and children lived there in bunk beds; sofa beds made of split bamboo (balé-balés) placed in two long rows. . . . The balé-balés in a row were divided using whatever people could find to create a semblance of privacy: an old sheet, old rags, some bamboo sticks on a rope used as a curtain, an old crate. One day, I had to wait a long time for my mother. She may have been held up doing some sort of chore. . . . I remember the situation very well: we had a two-story bunk bed some balé-balés away from an exit. The exit was blocked and children had to remain indoors. That would be the case when rabid dogs had been spotted in the camp. I had surely been worried about my mom not coming back, because we were very frightened about these rabid dogs. The women would walk in groups and carry sticks to defend themselves against them. It was not very bright outside, twilight was setting in. It must have been during the rainy season because I remember the humidity, but no great heat. I was sitting on the lower story of our balé-balé, near the aisle. There was no mattress and I felt the bamboo slats (concave on top with a slit in the middle). I was slouching and felt sad.
>
> When my mother arrived, I said: 'That took long, I was waiting eindelijk (finally).' She told me that I felt like I was waiting eindeloos (endlessly), and that she had arrived eindelijk (finally). She explained that eindeloos (endlessly) is something which does not seem to end, and that eindelijk (finally) means that something finally arrives or happens. First, I did not really get it and thought they were still the same, but she sat next to me on the lower half of the balé-balé, settled comfortably, and was sitting to the left of me when she explained it again and again, using slightly different words each time. And then I suddenly realized it, insight literally breaking through. Maybe not in a flash, but certainly like some sort of thunder. When I reflect on it (which I often do, because it is a memory that has stuck with me in some sort of pleasant manner), I think: 'Beng!, that was I when I knew.'"

Very different from the insight into the various definitions of certain abstract terms, such as used for the experience of time in the previous memory, is the realization that names are not natural properties of things – like they were born with them – but chosen by people from all sorts of options. A 47-year-old woman remembers the following:

> "I was six or seven years old. I had gone to play somewhere after school and my mother picked me up. It was already dark out and I

was sitting behind my mother on her bike. We were riding on an uneven road. Because it was already almost time for dinner, we were in a hurry. 'When we get home, we will sit down at the table immediately,' my mother said. I saw the set table in front of me. I captured the word 'table' in my mind. Suddenly, I realized that the word table had nothing to do with the object I had in my mind. I realized that you could easily call a table something different but that the thing itself would remain a table. I then thought about a knife, and the same applied. The knife in my mind remained a knife, even when I called it a fork, for example. Thinking about this made me giggle. I realized that people had created words for these things. Suddenly, I realized that everything had been given a word. I named the things I saw around me: 'bike', 'house', 'street'. I suddenly had the feeling that I understood the world. I was happy and delighted."

One can imagine that such insights into the relative nature of names for things are more likely and frequent in children who are raised bilingually or who are confronted with another language than their native one. A young woman wrote the following:

"I was five and a Dutch toddler when I entered the first grade of a French school. I had to learn to read there. There were letters below images of flowers and animals. It was incomprehensible to me, because even though I knew the letters and the meaning of those pictures, I did not know the words. Until the moment I saw a picture of a deer in front of me. I suddenly realized that I was expected to know the French word for 'deer', rather than the Dutch word 'hert'. This sudden insight is such a strong memory that I can still see myself sitting at that table, proud of myself that I had figured it out. I could read simple French shortly after this moment."

The memory of a friend of mine is also great. He lived in the city of Goes for the first 8 years of his life. When he returned to Goes as a young man, he walked the route he had often walked as a child with his mother from their home to visit friends. He remembered that he suddenly realized on one of these walks, around the age of 4, that he was not only called Rinus, but had another name, his last name: Ferdinandusse [last name DK]:

"We [mother and son DK] would walk on a curvy road, located higher up, past a lower one in a park. When visiting Goes and walking along the park I immediately recognized the scene: that is how

> we used to walk. And I also thought: 'Ah yes, that is the place where I suddenly realized that I was called Ferdinandusse.' I remember it as follows: 'Ferdinandusse? That is me'. . . . In all later conversations about Goes (usually memories of my father), I had seen everything in front of me, but not this. But when I walked there again, I knew it. I also remembered walking just off to the side of the stroller which would undoubtedly have contained my little brother Daan."

Rinus later offered a potential explanation. Before such visit, he was always told: 'Come on, we are going to Jeremiasse,' which was the last name of their friends. But once they arrived there, the friends were addressed using their first names, not as Jeremiasse. It seems like he suddenly combined these two names of their friends and thereafter applied it to his own name, because he will often have heard the name Ferdinandusse, without realizing that this also referred to him as well as Rinus.

14

SUDDEN COGNITIVE INSIGHTS

I have actually been interested in sudden insights in children since the start of my studies. However, I did not place it in the context of personality development, but of cognitive development. I will most certainly have been influenced by my grandfather Philip Kohnstamm, education professor at Amsterdam University.

In his ideas about the future of the Dutch education system, he was focused on acquiring insight, rather than on acquiring factual knowledge as taught by using drills.

In this context he was inspired by the impressive example of Helen Keller. She was an American woman, born in 1880, who became famous around the globe and of major importance to the emancipation of the blind and deaf.

She had become blind and deaf when she was 19 months old. As a result, she was unable to learn to speak and became an angry and unruly young child. When Helen became a toddler, her desperate parents entrusted her to the care of Annie Sullivan, who moved in with the family for this purpose. Annie turned out to be a loving, patient, and very intelligent governess.

Annie had been trying to teach Helen the names of everyday objects and daily actions by drawing letters with her finger on the palm of Helen's hand. Helen could not know that these were letters, but she must have experienced it as a mosaic of patterns. This is how she learned the patterns associated with touching a cup or a doll.

Annie Sullivan reported an event near the water pump in 1887 to her parents in a letter written on the very same day, which letter survived her.

After a violent scene during which Helen threw and broke a doll, Annie took her outside, to the pump house, and let water flow over Helen's hand, writing the signs for w-a-t-e-r in it. Helen was holding a cup in her other hand:

> "When this word immediately followed the experience of the cold water flowing over her hand, she seemed startled. She dropped the cup and stood frozen. A new light came over her face. She wrote 'water' in her own palm numerous times. She then dropped to the floor and showed that she wanted to know her name, and touched the pump and the lattice, turned around suddenly, and asked me about my name. I spelled 'teacher'. At that moment, the nanny brought Helen's little sister to the pump house and Helen spelled 'baby', pointing to the nanny. Returning to the large house, she was very excited and asked for the name of each object she touched. She learned thirty new words within a few hours this way. To name a few: door, open, closed, give, go, come, and many more."[1]

Helen suddenly realized that each object was associated with a unique combination of the same 26 separate signs. This is how she discovered the role of language. In her later autobiography, she wrote the following about this moment:

> "I suddenly felt a foggy awareness as if I had forgotten something – a vibration of a returning thought; and the mystery of language was revealed to me in an untraceable manner."[2]

This finger alphabet became the foundation for Helen's tumultuous development. She learned braille and graduated from the university cum laude. Her books and lectures in which she wrote and spoke about her ideas about how to deal with the deaf and blind led her to have a great impact.

There is an enormous gap between the sudden insight of Helen Keller and the insights 'regular' children may suddenly experience. But what happens at the moment itself is comparable. For example, the experience of being frozen in the moment, of having complete focus on the sudden change in one's own awareness, returns in many of the descriptions of memories I have received.

A few memories in my collection concern education. Both examples have to do with mathematics. A young woman described her discovery of the unit of measurement in the rods of Cuisenaire:

> "I am six years old and in a combined class in which children often work independently on subjects and assignments. I am doing mathematics, on the floor, using a sheet with calculations and the colored rods. The longest rod is orange and called 'ten', the second-longest is dark blue and called 'nine', all the way up to the smallest block, called 'one'. I was given the assignment of 'creating ten in various manners'. Below the rod called 'ten', I place smaller rods that together are just as long as 'ten'. A six and a four, for example. I then pick up a five to place another five below the ten, but accidentally pick up a six. Because the line is now too long, I first think: 'This is wrong.' Almost immediately afterwards, I realize that it is not 'wrong', but another calculation, and that you could 'go past ten'. I was overcome by a sense of surprise and elation. I picked up another 'ten' rod and another one and another and placed as many on the floor as I had available. I realized that I could go on like this and that these were units of measurement.
>
> Everything clicked in my mind within the span of a few seconds. It quietened me, and I will certainly have been staring out in the space in front of me for a while, noticing the bare treetops and realizing that these branches could also be divided into units of ten. I can remember the smell of the freshly cleaned linoleum, see the light of the TL lights in front of me, and feel the itchy white stockings I was wearing.
>
> I remember that the teacher came to check on me and asked what I was doing. I felt interrupted in my process of discovery and had difficulties explaining it; the fact that one could go past ten, that everything consisted of rods, that everything could be measured in this way. She confirmed this and I believe I remember that there was also a hint of appreciation. But I experienced it as a setback that 'I had to complete my sheet' and that 'calculations past ten would come later.'"

Poor child. The greatest ideal of Cuisenaire when creating his rods – or of Maria Montessori when designing her mathematical system using beads and rods – of a child independently coming to such insights through its own actions, turning on the light in his or her own mind, was considered as something disruptive by the teacher, who may have thought something like 'That's quite clever of that girl. But it simply not in line with the assignment she has to be working on'. Poor Cuisenaire.

Of course, the teacher can be excused. Children making major discoveries unfortunately do not have shining light bulbs above their heads. This would make it easier for parents and teachers to offer an adequate response. The woman who experienced this back when she was a 6-year-old girl adds the following to her memory:

> "I never became a great mathematician, but have always had a good spatial and geometric insight.
>
> Many years later, when our son was around five years old, we were visiting a flea market nearby, and that is where I found them, a box with Cuisenaire rods, my mathematical rods. 'I want those,' I thought, 'because he will begin learning mathematics soon, and could perhaps come to a similar kind of mathematical discovery.' I bought the box for 2. guiders. Back home, our son began playing with them. I remember thinking: 'See, it still works.' Until I brought him a glass of lemonade from the kitchen and was startled to discover that he had built a fort using the rods and had sheltered his soldiers behind a row of 'nines'. It seemed like heresy to me. 'Really fun blocks, mom,' he said."

These types of numerical insights must occur much more often than demonstrated in my collection of memories because I never asked for this kind of memories. I was focused solely on self-awareness, not on discoveries in general. It was my wife who saw a connection with the subject of this chapter when I told her what I was working on. She gave me this memory of her mathematical moment of insight:

> "I was seven years old and was learning the multiplication tables using cards the size of a large postcard. The tables of 1 to 10 were on one side, and those of 11 to 20 on the other. A new table was added every week, and we had to recite out loud together the tables we had already covered at least twice every day, as was the case in front-facing instruction back in the day. I can see myself sitting there holding the card in my hand. Apparently, we are starting with a new table. I can no longer remember which one, but I think it was the table of eight, because that is what I was looking at. A light-brown card with black figures. I can see myself sitting on the bench in the

> second row from the window, in the middle, on the left side of the two-person bench. I saw 7x8=56. I thought: hey, 8x7 is also 56! And I understood the mathematical system in a flash."

There are psychologists and educationalists who believe that insights obtained independently by a child are more valuable than insights obtained through instructions, examples, and explanation by older persons. But there are just as many, if not more, people who believe that one should not wait too long for independent discoveries, and that it is more efficient to teach these insights to whole classes of children as possible.

My grandfather pursued the independent insights. In the field of cognitive psychology, he witnessed the introduction of the so-called 'Gestaltpsychology' and saw in it a revolution in the ideas about human cognition and the corresponding meaning of this for education. Enabling people to come to their own insights should be promoted as much as possible in this field. That was his educational ideal.

A Gestalt is a whole that the brain constructs from a number of separate elements coming in through the sensory organs.

In the course of human evolution, our brains have obtained an increasingly greater capacity to turn perceptions of individual elements into meaningful wholes at lightning speed and then deliver them to our consciousness. It is only afterward that we can deliberately start to focus on the elements. This is how our brains have access to an incalculable arsenal of objects, situations, facial expressions, and what not, which they can immediately introduce to our consciousness. The first 'law' of the Gestalt psychology is therefore 'The whole precedes the parts'.

For example, consider how you perceive a landscape after you have climbed a mountain and are taking in the valley below all at once. Or how you look at a painting that you are seeing for the first time: you will first get an impression of the overall picture. You will only afterward study the incidence of light or the brush strokes. Or how you register a hazardous traffic situation. Particularly in this scenario it is almost a blessing that you can first take in the overall picture before noticing and processing the individual elements of the situation.

But the surprising thing about our brains is that they anyway attempt to establish the whole from a collection of individual elements, including *wholes* that do not already 'exist'. Our brains are focused on constructing – within the blink of an eye – a meaningful whole from a range of perceptions that in a purely physical sense are not related but which are, possibly accidentally, presented to the observer at the same time. Observing as we consciously experience it is not a passive process of receiving stimuli on our retinas, on the skin, making our eardrums vibrate, but our brains are focused on turning these into a meaningful whole. This is where the second 'law' of Gestaltpsychologie stems from: 'The whole is more than the sum of its parts', as the elements that are meaningless in itself are given a useful meaning when merged. This process leads to a new insight. 'Hey, you can go past ten'. 'Hey, I can lie'. 'Hey, I am I'.

No wonder that philosophers and psychologists have become fascinated by the sudden breakthrough of new insights – because this is where the key to progress can be found. Are not many inventions based on brains that came to a sudden restructuring of elements that were interpreted completely different by everyone up to that point? This is how sudden insights break through, how people get ideas. In our consciousness they appear as sudden, but in our brain they are probably preceded by preparing steps.

We also continue to gain sudden insights into our personal lives, insights into our relationships, for example. How these have gradually changed. And how we suddenly realize this. By way of an example, I wish to quote the English philosopher Bertrand Russell from his autobiography:

> "I went for a bike ride that afternoon and was riding on a country road, when I suddenly realized that I no longer loved Alys. I had not been aware of a loss of my love for her beforehand at all, up to this moment."[3]

Our brain picks up all kinds of minuscule signals in our semi-conscious thoughts and turns these into a whole. That is when conscious insight comes, which insight we can explore in our mind and express to ourselves and for others.

I will use the last chapter to present one of the latest developments in neuroscience that may in the future reveal something about which processes in our brain can lead to sudden insight about ourselves and our relations with others around us.

Notes

1 Ann Sullivan Macy (1933) *The Story Behind Helen Keller.* New York, Doran Doubleday.
2 Helen Keller (1909) *The Story of My Life.* New York, Random House.
3 Bertrand Russell (1968) *Autobiography.* London, George Allan and Unwin.

15

A MIND-WANDERING NETWORK

We generally tend to think that our brain has 'time off', is in a passive state, when we have no tasks to perform. This is indeed the case for specialized areas in the cerebral cortex, such as the speech center, the visual center, or the motor center. Around the last turn of the century, scientists in the United States discovered that there are nervous networks that become precisely more active when people are resting. This was a major discovery in the field of our brains and the way we think, especially about ourself.

It was an example of so-called serendipitous or accidental discovery.

A scientist or a group of scientists is studying a certain phenomenon and suddenly they see something interesting that seemingly has nothing to do with their research object. By this way, Alexander Fleming discovered the principle of penicillin when he saw something strange had happened in a moldy test tube. And Wilhelm Röntgen accidentally saw that the bones of his hand lit up through a metal plate he had smeared with a chemical.[1]

A group of neuropsychologists researched which areas of the brain were involved in the performance of various tasks. The test subjects were lying in an fMRI scanner with electrodes on their heads. At some point, the researchers saw that one network area that had not participated became active when the subjects were resting after a task. At first this was seen as a somewhat disturbing error in the experimental procedure. But the scientific curiosity was triggered and finally it emerged as a mainstream target of study.

This discovery led in the first quarter of our twenty-first century to an incredibly large succession of research projects in universities all over the

Western world and in China. Quite a lot is now known about this network, which is composed of three connected brain areas.

The English-language Wikipedia carries a very elaborate article with illuminating illustrations. It begins with: 'It is a large-scale brain network best known for being active when a person is not focused on the outside world and the brain is in wakeful rest [i.e., not sleeping DK] such as during daydreaming and mind-wandering.'[2]

The name for this network that was coined by the head of the research group Marcus Raichle is Default Mode Network (DMN), also shortened to Default Network.

At first, I thought this to be a somewhat unfortunate name, 'default' having all kinds of unfavorable meanings. In Webster's I found meanings as 'Failure to do something required by duty or law'; 'Failure to pay financial debts'; 'Failure to finish an appointed contest'. However, this network is anything but a failure; it turns out to be essential for human consciousness.

I told Professor Raichle about my problem in a mail correspondence. He was very surprised: "Nobody else had expressed such a complaint to him before".

Shortly thereafter, I noticed that Webster's newest *digital* edition had added a brand-new meaning for 'default': 'A selection automatically used by a program in the absence of a choice made by the user'. This meaning of 'default' stems from the language spoken by people who design computer programs. For example, a user forgets or fails to give an answer to a question posed by the program or skips this question intentionally. In these cases, the program gives a standard reaction. It is in a 'default mode'; it remains on standby and becomes in action as soon as the user presses a key to start an exercise.

When I informed Marcus Raichle about this new meaning, he answered enthusiastically: 'Dear Dolph, I like it! It captures the essence of how I was thinking when I penned the title of our 2001 paper *Default Mode of Brain Function*'.[3]

So, in the same way, the Default Network is always on standby and comes in action only when a person is in an inner-directed mode, not focused on external tasks but lets his or her thoughts wander. It is, in other words, in a type of wandering state and that's why for this book a 'mind-wandering network' is a good name. It is also often mentioned in research articles to explain DMN's most typical mindset for new readers.

The same difference was for instance found between two different meditation methods: ACEM and directive. ACEM is non-directive, and thoughts can wander freely. With this method, the Default Network is activated, more than with the directive method.[4] In the directive method, the subjects get the assignment to concentrate well, for instance, on their breathing.

Many people get ideas and find solutions when not deliberately looking for them, but when they are 'simply letting their mind wander'. A great saying by Albert Einstein:

> "I never came upon any of my discoveries through the process of rational thinking."

What was happening in the brain of this great scholar when he made a discovery is essentially the same as what happened in the mind of the 6-year-old girl in this book when she was busy with the Cuisenaire blocks and by an accidental 'error' discovered that 'one could go past ten'.

In this connection, Raichle wrote to me:

> "I will bet that 'rational thinking' and its attendant 'mental effort' involves attenuating the role of DMN. I have often thought about this in the context of that 'pop out memory' which is exemplified by unexpectedly meeting someone you know but whose name you can't remember (embarrassing). It is only sometime later when you have moved on and shed the embarrassment of forgetting their name that it mysteriously 'pops out'."

The Default Network is a node at the front of the cerebral cortex in which nerve endings from areas of the brain that are sometimes far apart merge to share and communicate signals.

The network is highly active when a person is in an inward-looking mood, when self-consciousness is involved; it is far less active when he or she is busy with external tasks that are cognitive demanding and need attention and concentration.

The importance of the inner-directed mode is expressed in the given that the energy consumption when the 'Self' is concerned is far higher than during activations driven by external stimulation. When the Default Network is active, the metabolism in the brain is in balance, but as soon as the person shifts his or her attention from internally oriented to externally oriented tasks and incentives, this balance is disturbed. That's why the state of the Default Network is also called the 'normal' or 'baseline' state of mind.

The two different states alternate in what Antonio Damasio has called 'a seesaw pattern' regarding the role of the Self. He also uses a dance metaphor:

> "It possibly reflects the background-foreground dance played by the Self within de conscious mind. When we need to attend to external

> stimuli, our conscious mind brings the object under scrutiny into the foreground and lets the Self retreat into the background. When we are unsolicited by the outside world our Self moves closer to center stage and may even move further forward when the object under scrutiny is our own person, alone or in its social setting."[5]

When the Self is facing itself, it reflects on, among other things, memories, what it expects to do in the future, thinking about consequences of social decisions it might need to take, especially in issues involving morality.

But the mood in which the greatest activity is shown in the Default Network of a person is when he or she gives himself or herself assignments that are related to our empathic skills, related to the question of 'how would I feel in that situation?' This network is not only active when thinking about ourselves, but also when we try to put ourselves into someone else's shoes. This last aspect is called '*theory of mind*'. It can be considered as the ability to come to a theory on what another person is thinking about things that are also of concern to yourself. Therefore the network is, by some researchers, also named 'the social network' or 'the social brain'.

For the first time in the history of neuroscience, the probability that self-awareness comes from activities in the Default Network of our brain has been demonstrated.

The Dutch neurologist Dick Swaab mentioned an experiment that enhanced this probability.

> "The activity in our Default Network reacts differently to hearing our own name compared to someone else's and our 'self' which is thereby created allows for conscious experiences. The following experiment supports this idea. An eminent singer was made to listen to Mozart arias in an fMRI scanner which had either been sung by herself or by an other singer. The difference in her brain activity indicated that cortical midline structures (where the network is located [DK]) are involved in the sense of self, in this case with the singer's identity."[6]

With these new neuropsychological insights in our minds, we return to the memories in my collection about sudden self-awareness. Why did I include a chapter on this network in this book? Because all the remembered moments of self-awareness can very well be products from the DMN.

Many of them took place when the children were not doing anything. They were lying half-awake in bed. They were overwhelmed by nature.

They were walking the well-known road between home and school. They were simply staring into the void petulantly. Or they were standing in the sunlight. In short, they were in a mind-wandering state.

My assumption is that sudden experiences of self-awareness can arise when a child is in such a state that activates the inner-directed mode of the Default Network.

But is this network already sufficiently developed in children?

Recent research has shown that even in 1-year-old children, there is network connectivity demonstrable.[7] But as long as the language development is insufficient to catch such experiences in words, there can be no memory of self-awareness in later life. So, my next assumption is that only precocious children in terms of language development can have an experience of self-awareness to remember. I gave already a few examples of very young children (the girl sitting on the veranda on the island of Ceram and the girl lying in bed and listening to the crackling of her brother's swing).

To sustain these assumptions, I present three experiences of 3- and 4-year-olds.

A middle-aged Swiss woman, a translator and psychology student, remembers:

Not these clothes!

"It was morning and I had just woken up. I took the clothes that my mother had put out for me. I looked at these clothes and thought: Not these! I don't want to wear these clothes. The moment is very clear in my memory: I am different from her; I don't ever want to be the same as her; she has no idea who I am; I'll wear what I want! I couldn't and wouldn't wear these clothes, and picked out what I wanted myself. I felt very clearly that I was my own person with individual (of course I did not yet know that word) desires. On the one hand, I felt very strong at that moment; on the other, I also felt somewhat sad and alone."

A young German woman wrote:

In the wading pool

"It must have been summertime. I was just sitting there on the steps in the water of the wading pool at the municipal swimming center. My hair was wet. As I could tell from later pictures, this was my favourite thing to do: to put my hair in the water. The first thing that I noticed was the light blue color of the swimming pool, and the drain I was sitting close to. And then there was this feeling that I could remove myself from the crowd, from the confusion of voices around me – suddenly have my own world. I didn't exactly think 'Hey I am somebody ', but I could distinguish myself from others. This experience has remained vividly in my memory, even today. So now, when I close my eyes, I can still hear this confusion of voices around me, the moment of the feeling I had at that moment still makes me smile. Perhaps I also smiled at the time."

A young German student majoring in Asian Studies describes the following scene:

In the family car

"We were driving to my grandparents' house. I had three older brothers and we always had to fit six people in the car, which actually only had enough room and seatbelts for five. So I often stood between the two front seats in order to not be cramped and to get a better view of the road. As we were travelling through a village, I was suddenly overcome with exactly this feeling, that I had just discovered myself – my 'I'. I started to repeat my name to myself (I don't remember if I said this inwardly or out loud): Ca-ro-lin Yes I am Carolin. I repeated my name over and over, and in doing so became more conscious of myself. This state lasted until we had driven through the village."

The pattern that emerges in research literature is that in general the Default Network regions are beginning to function from 7 years on, with a spurt in early adolescence (13–14 years old) to be fully developed at age 21.

This book contains 107 memories collected by me; 81 of these originate from when the children were between 7 and 15 years old. Most of them again (55) are from children who were between 7 and 10 years old when the language development is in full swing.

So, I think the conclusion is justified that the experiences of sudden self-awareness as described in this book in children under 10 years of age are produced by their earlier than average maturating Default Networks.

That I got far more memories from women than from men suggests that in all age groups, the maturation of the DMN function is faster for girls than for boys.[8]

As a final point: I believe that just like all other human brain functions, the Default Mode Network must be a product of human evolution, including cultural evolution.

Notes

1 Randy L. Buckner (2012) The serendipitous discovery of the brain's default network. *NeuroImage*, volume 62, issue 2.

Svend Davanger (2015) The brain's default network: What does it mean to us? Interview with Marcus Raichle. *ACEM Meditation Blog*, March 9th.

2 Wikipedia, Default mode network.

3 Marcus E. Raichle et al. (2001) A default mode of brain function. *Proceedings of the Academy of Sciences of the United States of America*, volume 98, issue 2.

4 V.A. Taylor et al. (2012) Impact of meditation training on the default mode network during restful state. *Social Cognitive and Affective Neuroscience*, March 24th.

5 Antonio Damasio (2010) *Self Comes to Mind: Constructing the Conscious Brain.* New York, Pantheon Books.

6 Dick Swaab (2016) *Our Creative Brains.* Amsterdam, Atlas Contact Uitgeverij.

7 Wei Gao (2009) Evidence on the emergence of the brain's default network from 2-week-old to 2-year-old healthy pediatric subjects. *Proceedings of the Academy of Sciences of the United States of America*, volume 106, issue16.

8 Keila Rebello et al. (2018) Default mode network maturation and environmental adversities during childhood. *Neuroscience, Neurology & Psychiatry Online*, November 14th.

16
CODA

Evidently, I was forced to select out of all memories given or sent to me over the course of about 30 years.

During the first selection, I put examples of 'first' or 'earliest' memories aside. These have another significance than sudden insights.

Memories that were described in overly adult terms, which included thoughts a child of the age in question would certainly not have, were also put aside.

The second selection was for practical reasons: the size of the book. I did not include certain memories because I had sufficient good examples of certain types of experiences.

Where necessary, I have made minor editorial changes to the letters included in this book but never made changes to their contents.

It is interesting that about 80 percent of all responses I received came from women. I have three down-to-earth explanations for this.

It can partly be attributed to the fact that I published my requests in magazines that are mainly read by women.

It could also be that men felt ashamed to write to me about such 'childish thoughts'. Or would a request in a magazine aimed at men not have been published at all? The majority of the memories found in literature, however, are written by men.

Finally, it could be because more women than men are interested in psychological topics, just as girls make up the majority of psychology students.

But there is more to say. I ended the last chapter with the suggestion that the development of the Default Network function could be faster for girls than for boys, making the possibility of inner speech – a prerequisite for self-awareness – earlier.

Girls in general surpass boys in language development and research has shown that women are generally better able to remember events from their childhood than men. This is sometimes explained by the fact that parents discuss events and the corresponding emotions more often with their daughters. Young girls are also better able to remember more from the past than young boys. They can also tell more about these events, such as the precise time and place of the event, and the associated emotions.[1]

One question you could ask yourself after reading this book concerns the later significance of such self-insight for children.

I have not studied this. But I have the impression that for the majority of the people who have written to me about such an event, it is no more than a valuable souvenir without any emotional impact. In some people, for whom the event was associated with fear for the sudden loneliness, the memory still invokes the same fear, but not severely or traumatically.

There are also people for whom the memory of their I-am-I experience has always remained associated with a proud feeling of having discovered something important, a sense of autonomy and of being in control. In times of need, they fall back on this memory and draw strength from it. In difficult times, they may find solace in the memory of that moment.

And what about the major question: Did it really happen or not?

I can only answer that the way in which the memories have been described give me a sense of authenticity, of raw purity. I do not have any other proof of what is 'real' than this feeling. There is no proof.

But I feel supported by my former Dutch colleague, Professor Willem Albert Wagenaar, a specialist in memories, who often had to assess the reliability of statements as an expert witness in legal proceedings.

According to him, there are memories from childhood that offer a correct, authentic representation of what happened at the time. Not all childhood memories are distorted and changed during the course of a life.

Psychologists who serve as expert witnesses in legal proceedings concerning sexual abuse employ a number of assessment criteria. One of these is the level of detail in the description of the situation during which the abusive conduct took place. They pay special attention to details that are irrelevant to this conduct, such as the color of the wallpaper, the stain on the curtain, the creaking door. This irrelevance contributes to a sense of believability. But the same applies here: sense, not evidence.

The memories in this book contain many 'irrelevant' details. Imperfections in the railing, sunlight hitting a tree, green satin chairs, the door spring on the top of a door, a height difference between the sidewalk and the street, a porcelain angel on the wall. To me, such details enhance the authenticity of the memory.

Another assessment criterion in legal proceedings is the level-headedness with which a person talks about the memory. When selecting the letters, I have left out cases in which I had doubts about the authenticity because the memories were described in overly lofty terms. A sober simplicity was missing in them.

One question I ask myself is whether such sudden I-am-I experiences can nowadays still occur. Is there still room for childlike self-reflection? A lot of semi-psychological conversations take place with and around children. People talk with them a lot about what they are thinking and feeling. Each child's question must be answered with an attitude of understanding: listen to your child! Children are no longer given mental rest. They seem to be encouraged to think about themselves by well-intentioned adults. Sudden insight seems to be reserved for children whose thoughts can develop in peace without the need for ongoing communication about these thoughts. I hope that parents who read this book will not ask their children whether they feel like an 'I', or if they 'have ever thought about this'!

Dear reader,

If you happen to have a memory dating from your childhood years or school-age years, as described in this book, I would welcome a description of that memory! Include as many details as possible, the surrounding circumstances, and your best estimation of your age at that memorable moment.

Please send your memory to ritakohnstamm@mac.com.

Note

1 Robyn Fivush (1998) Gendered narratives: Elaboration, structure, and emotion in parent-child reminiscing across the preschool years. In Charles P. Thompson et al. *Autobiographical Memory*. Mahwah, NJ, Erlbaum.

INDEX

For Product Safety Concerns and Information please contact our EU
representative GPSR@taylorandfrancis.com
Taylor & Francis Verlag GmbH, Kaufingerstraße 24, 80331 München, Germany

www.ingramcontent.com/pod-product-compliance
Ingram Content Group UK Ltd.
Pitfield, Milton Keynes, MK11 3LW, UK
UKHW022109190926
475702UK00013B/1334

* 9 7 8 0 3 6 7 7 5 2 0 4 0 *